REFORMATION AND
CATHOLICITY

REFORMATION
AND CATHOLICITY

by GUSTAF AULÉN

translated by ERIC H. WAHLSTROM

OLIVER AND BOYD
EDINBURGH & LONDON

OLIVER AND BOYD LTD
Tweeddale Court
Edinburgh

39a Welbeck Street
London, W.1
1962

Translated by Eric H. Wahlstrom from the original
Swedish edition, *Reformation och Katolicitet,* published by the Svenska Kyrkans Diakonistyrelses Bok-
förlag in Stockholm, 1959.

Printed in Great Britain by
John Dickens & Conner Ltd. Northampton

PREFACE

The Reformation was the most profound rupture in the life of Christendom. For this reason it quite naturally becomes an object of special attention in this age of ecumenical endeavors. The point of departure for what is presented here has been the lively debate concerning the Reformation which has been going on in recent times, not least of all the remarkable contributions coming from prominent Roman theologians. The opinions they have presented show features obviously divergent from the stereotyped controversies of the past. Their estimate of the Reformation is, from some central points of view, entirely positive. In other respects however, their criticisms have hardened. The analysis of such documents could not be performed without an analysis of the Reformation itself. The Reformation did not intend to create "a new church." It emphasized forcefully that the reformed church was a continuation of the apostolic church, of that church which in the Creed is described as "one, holy, and catholic." In the history of the reformed church this view of the Reformation has not always been maintained. In this book I have tried to examine the meaning and the rightfulness of "catholicity" as vindicated by the Reformation, and also the demands implicit in it for church life today. Hence it was necessary to investigate the confession of the Reformation and its relationship to the biblical confession and the confessions of the ancient church, as well as its conception of "tradition" as expressed in doctrine, liturgy, and church order. My intention has not been to write an apology of all that happened in the Reformation, still less of all that has happened in the history of the reformed church. It has rather been to explain what was really nuclear in the Reformation achievement, with a hope that such an explanation could further in some degree the matter-of-factness of the conversations between the churches going on in the ecumenical age.

The Swedish edition of this book appeared in the spring of 1959.

Lund, November 1960   GUSTAF AULÉN

CONTENTS

REFORMATION AND
CATHOLICITY

CHAPTER 1

ESTIMATES OF THE REFORMATION IN THE AGE OF ECUMENICITY

1. INTRODUCTION

Christendom has experienced many schisms during its history of almost two thousand years. These schisms began with the christological conflicts in the days of the ancient church. Two of these schisms were especially significant: the separation between East and West which, after a series of conflicts that began back in the ninth century, was finally completed in A.D. 1054; and the division associated with the Reformation in the sixteenth century.

When we compare these two schisms, it is obvious that the second caused the more thoroughgoing separation. The reason was that the antithesis created at that time involved central religious and theological concerns. It is true that to some extent the opposition between Rome and Byzantium had to do with dogmatic and cultic questions, but it was at the same time largely a power conflict between the two great centers of Christendom at that time. Even the Reformation conflict became gradually combined with a political struggle. In the beginning, however, it was a question about antitheses which belong entirely in the sphere of religious and theological concern, and which were much more profound than those which separated Rome and Byzantium.

Under these circumstances it is obvious that the ecumenical discussions about "faith and order" cannot avoid dealing with the Reformation. If the purpose of ecumenical efforts is to further mutual Christian fellowship and to manifest externally

1

the unity of Christendom, the ecumenical discussions cannot fail to consider those factors which in the course of time have caused separations, especially the Reformation and its position within Christendom.

The first chapter will deal with the various attitudes toward the Reformation in modern times. Our concern is primarily with those churches which either stood outside of the Reformation conflict, or which became the object of the Reformation attack; i.e., the Eastern Orthodox church and Rome. In this connection, therefore, we may ignore those churches which were directly involved in the Reformation. An exception must be made, however, with respect to the Anglican church. This church occupies a unique position insofar as it wants to represent a *via media* and to unite a "Catholic" and a Reformation tradition in a synthesis. In reference to Anglicanism we must pay particular attention to the criticism the "Anglo-Catholic" faction has levelled against the Reformation. Finally there are some reasons why we must consider the post-Reformation Methodist and Baptist churches, both of which in different ways show a divergence from the Reformation.

Rome has not officially participated in the modern ecumenical discussions. At some of the ecumenical conferences observers from the Roman communion have been present. But while the Vatican has always protested its profound interest in everything that may further the unity of the church, it has consistently declined all invitations to participate directly in ecumenical meetings and discussions. This attitude, however, has not prevented Roman theologians from being intensively engaged in ecumenical debates. It is even true that in modern times the question we are discussing here—the attitude to the Reformation—has not been the object of such intensive study anywhere as among Roman theologians. What they have written is of such a remarkable nature that we must pay special attention to it. Among the numerous works which might be considered in this connection, I have selected a few mainly from French authors. I have not attempted a comprehensive review of the literature in this field.

2. *THE EASTERN ORTHODOX CHURCH*

The Eastern Orthodox church was represented from the time the smaller, preparatory ecumenical meetings were held in Geneva during the summer of 1920, which became the starting point for the great conferences in Stockholm in 1925 (Life and Work) and in Lausanne in 1927 (Faith and Order). At Geneva the Orthodox delegates presented a document from the Patriarch of Constantinople in which he expressed his interest in the cause and outlined a program for future co-operation. From that time on the Orthodox church has been represented in the ecumenical deliberations, but political factors have been the chief reason for the representation being severely limited. For obvious reasons the Russian church has never been able to send any delegates. It has been represented only by emigrant churchmen and theologians. In spite of their earlier participation the Orthodox churches in the Balkan states, nations now behind "the iron curtain" and within the Soviet orbit, have in general been prevented from attending.

Under these circumstances the number of Orthodox representatives has been relatively small. But this representation has been of immense significance, especially from the point of view of principle. Their presence, together with representatives from some of the smaller oriental churches, separated from the rest during the time of the ancient church, and in addition delegates from the Old Catholic church, has given a comprehensive character to the ecumenical conferences which they would not have had if the delegates had come only from the churches directly involved in the Reformation. But no less significant have been the important scholarly contributions of the Orthodox theologians to the ecumenical debate.

At the conclusion of the small conference in Geneva in 1920, where the first meeting with Orthodox churchmen took place, the chairman, Bishop Charles H. Brent of the Protestant Episcopal church in the United States, spoke with poetic fervor of the significance of contact with the Orthodox church and its worship life. The background of his words was the fact that on the last day of the conference the delegates had been invited to attend the festal worship in the Russian church in Geneva.

The Bishop said: "We of the West need the fragrant, graceful worship of the East. The beauty of God filled his temple. We felt that we had been drawn within the pearly gates of the Apocalypse, and we came away with *pain bénit* and grapes in our hands, and sweetness in our souls, under the spell of the mystic East."

To this pronouncement from the first period of the ecumenical movement we may add another from more recent times. In *The Ecumenical Review*, 1958, Professor E. Schlink wrote an article describing how ecumenical association with the Orthodox church has gradually given many members of the Reformation churches a new conception of this church and its worship life.[1] Schlink, as well as Brent, emphasizes the liturgical aspect. Dogma in the Eastern church, he says, is determined by the structure of doxology. In contrast to earlier criticism voiced in many quarters that the Orthodox church has been at a standstill, Schlink speaks of "its decided disinclination to formulate new dogmas" as something healthy. The Eastern church has a greater respect for "the mystery of redemption" than the Western. Schlink maintains that this dogmatic reticence implies great ecumenical possibilities especially if the matter is seen from the point of view of liturgy and preaching.

We have listened to a couple of voices speaking of contact with the Orthodox church. Without question this church has appeared to many of the participants in the ecumenical movement as a more or less strange body, both fascinating and repelling. But however the opinions may vary, in any case it remains true that the ancient church tradition appears as a living reality in the Orthodox church in a way quite different from that found in other communions. It does not appear as an inheritance dragged along from the dim past, but precisely as a living reality. In this connection I would call attention not only to the doxological conception of the confession but also and especially to the dominant position of Easter and the resurrection in the worship life and theology of the Orthodox church. Not least in

[1] "Changes in Protestant Thinking about the Eastern Church," *The Ecumenical Review*, July, 1958, pp. 386ff.

this respect, the Eastern church has an important message to bring forth in the ecumenical context.

The Orthodox church was not actively involved when the Reformation tempest swept over western Christendom. Consequently it had no occasion to define its attitude to either the Lutheran or the Calvinistic Reformation. Its present attitude to the Reformation, therefore, is not hampered by earlier decisions, while Rome's attitude is more fixed because of its official repudiation of the movement at the Council of Trent. But even if the Orthodox church to some extent occupies a less encumbered position, its certainty that both in doctrine and cult as well as in the general structure of the church it represents the "true" church must make it predisposed to adopt a reserved attitude toward other communions. The actions of Orthodox churchmen manifest both of these positions. They are uninhibited by the controversies of the Reformation, but they also at times present a rigid posture.

The most definite expression of a positive attitude to the Reformation message appears in a pronouncement by the Conference in Edinburgh (1937) concerning "The Grace of our Lord Jesus Christ." The statement emphasizes *sola gratia* and gives a clear expression to the message which was the central concern of the Reformation. I quote some important sentences. "Man's salvation and welfare have their source in God alone, who is moved to His gracious activity towards man not by any merit or man's part, but solely by His free, outgoing love." "God in his free, outgoing love justifies and sanctifies us through Christ, and his grace thus manifested is appropriated by faith, which itself is the gift of God. Justification and sanctification are two inseparable aspects of God's gracious action in dealing with sinful man." [2] This document, as I personally know very well, was worked out in close co-operation between Lutheran and Orthodox theologians, and it was the only one accepted unanimously by the Conference. In an introductory statement the Conference expressed its thankfulness for this result. "With deep thankful-

---

[2] Leonard Hodgson (ed.), *The Second World Conference on Faith and Order, Edinburgh, 1937* (New York, 1938), p. 224. Hereafter referred to as *Edinburgh, 1937.*

ness to God for the spirit of unity, which by His gracious blessing upon us has guided and controlled all our discussions on this subject, we agree on the following statement and recognize that there is in connection with this subject no ground for maintaining divisions between churches."

It is easy to understand why the Roman theologian Thomas Sartory characterizes this agreement on the subject of grace as "astonishing" (*erstaunlich*). At the same time he quotes another Roman theologian, J. P. Michael, who says that the agreement must be considered important because "here a *virus protestanticus* has been eliminated." [3] This interpretation is obviously an attempt to explain why the agreement was possible at all. The background of such an interpretation, however, seems to be the traditional misunderstanding of the *sola gratia* of the Reformation, namely, the conception that *sola gratia* must exclude all human activity.

The agreement mentioned here concerns a question of vital importance. In other areas, however, the Orthodox representatives have generally shown great reluctance to participate in decisions and pronouncements. They have often registered dissenting opinions. The chief reason for this reluctance is their fundamental conception of the Orthodox church and its relationship to other churches, viz., their conviction that the only possible basis of church unity is for other churches to return to or even be absorbed into the Eastern church.

We must note first some reservations the Orthodox churchmen have added to pronouncements of the conferences. The report of the conference in Edinburgh contains a statement about "The Communion of Saints." The Orthodox delegates have added the following dissenting declaration. We "hold that the mother of our Lord, designated as 'Theotokos' (God-bearer), the ever-Virgin, should be venerated as the highest of all saints and angels, and of all creation. In addition to the general recognition of the Communion of Saints, we venerate particular

---

[3] Thomas Sartory, *Die oekumenische Bewegung und die Einheit der Kirche* (1954), pp. 34-35. Cf. G. H. Tavard, *The Catholic Approach to Protestantism* (New York: Harper, 1955).

saints who are honored by the church, and ask their intercession and that of the angels before God." [4]

In the chapter about "Ministry and Sacraments" the conference had formulated the following sentence: "All church tradition regarding the sacraments ought to be controlled and tested by Scripture." A footnote says: "The Orthodox and some others would wish to add: 'All the sacraments can be founded upon Holy Scripture as completed, explained, interpreted and understood in the Holy Tradition by the guidance of the Holy Spirit residing in the Church." [5]

Concerning the Eucharist the Orthodox delegates added the following separate statement: "a) The Orthodox church believes and teaches that in the Sacrament of the Holy Eucharist, which is the extension of the only and once offered sacrifice of our Lord, the offered gifts by virtue of the consecration are changed (*metaballontai*) into the very Body and the very Blood of our Lord Jesus Christ, and given to the faithful for the remission of sins and life everlasting. b) The Holy Eucharist can be celebrated only by a validly ordained minister." [6]

The Conference on Faith and Order in Lund (1952) dealt with the following four questions: 1) Christ and his Church, 2) Continuity and Unity, 3) Ways of Worship, 4) Intercommunion. In the reports of the commissions several different opinions were expressed, usually with the formula, "some would say—others say." The conference discussed the reports, but no decision was made except that the reports as a whole were "received *nemine contradicente*" and commended to the churches for consideration. The following statement was added: "The delegates representing the Orthodox churches under the jurisdiction of the Ecumenical Patriarchate had taken part in the Conference in expounding the Orthodox view both in section meetings and in plenary sessions, but took no part in the voting upon the reception of the Report." [7] The cautious position of the Orthodox church was thus quite forcefully emphasized.

---

[4] *Edinburgh, 1937*, p. 15.
[5] *Ibid.*, p. 18.
[6] *Ibid.*, p. 23.
[7] *Report of the Third World Conference on Faith and Order, Lund, 1952*, p. 51. Hereafter referred to as *Lund, 1952*.

Now that we have indicated how the Orthodox delegates have demonstrated their positive interest in ecumenical discussions, but at the same time have manifested a very cautious attitude, we must also consider some Orthodox pronouncements about the Reformation. We find a very instructive document in an article written by one of the most prominent Orthodox theologians, Professor G. Florovsky. This article was a contribution to *Intercommunion,* a book published as a study guide in preparation for the conference in Lund.[8]

The purpose of this frank paper is to explain why the Orthodox church rejects eucharistic fellowship with other churches. Florovsky is fully aware that such a position may easily be considered rigid, intransigent, and a token of extreme confessionalism. He considers it absolutely necessary, however, that ecumenical deliberations not conceal or cover up existing antitheses, or ignore matters of conscience. At the close of the article Florovsky states clearly why he regards this question as a matter of conscience. He is convinced that the Orthodox church "is in very truth *the Church,* i.e., *the true Church* and the only true Church. I believe this," he says, "for many reasons: by personal conviction and by inner testimony of the Spirit which breathes in the sacraments of the Church and by all that I could learn from Scripture and from the universal tradition of the church. I am compelled therefore to regard all other Christian Churches as deficient, and in many cases I can identify these deficiencies accurately enough." His conclusion is: "For me Christian reunion is just universal conversion to Orthodoxy. I have no confessional loyalty; my loyalty belongs solely to the *Una Sancta.*"

The point of the argumentation is that since the Orthodox church is the only true Church, his confessional loyalty should not be regarded as factional. But Florovsky adds some restrictions and explanations to his statement that the Orthodox church is the only true church. First of all he does not mean "that everything in the past or present state of the Orthodox Church is to

---

[8] G. Florovsky, "Confessional Loyalty in the Ecumenical Movement," in D. M. Baillie and J. Marsh (eds.), *Intercommunion,* the Report of the Theological Commission Appointed by the Continuation Committee of the World Conference on Faith and Order (New York: Harper, 1952), pp. 196-205.

be equated with the truth of God. Many things are obviously changeable; indeed many things need improvement. The *true* Church is not the perfect Church." "Revision and restatement is always possible, sometimes imperative." Yet "on the whole" the deposit has been faithfully kept and, above all, the sacramental structure of the church has been kept integral and intact. In the second place, the claim to be the only true church does not "unchurch those who do not belong to the Catholic Church of history. The most rigid 'Catholic' will regard all faithful Christians as related, in some sense to be defined, or even as belonging, to the Church of Christ. . . . The true composition of the Church is known to the Lord of the Church only."

When Florovsky turns his attention to the "Protestants" (he puts "Catholic" and "Protestant" within quotation marks), he suggests that "Protestants," if they are consistent, must think about their churches in the same way as he himself does about the Orthodox church. They must claim that the churches of the Reformation are representatives of a true kind of church, and that no church can be true unless it has gone through a process of reformation more or less similar to that of the sixteenth century. "Unreformed means in this connection exactly untrue." The consequence would be that "Protestants" cannot allow intercommunion with "Catholics," because they consider the belief in the sacrifice of the Mass a corruption and an erroneous doctrine.

Florovsky then raises the question as to whether the Reformation was a gain or a loss—a forward step, or a step in the wrong direction. Such a question, he says, cannot be answered without a painstaking analysis, which he is unable to undertake within the limits of his paper. He supplies an answer, however, insofar as he summarily indicates his objections to the Reformation. The first objection concerns the doctrine of the sacraments, and especially the negative attitude of the Reformation to the sacramental sacrifice. The same objection is underscored by another Orthodox theologian, L. Zander, who contributed an article entitled "Intercommunion and Co-celebration." [9] He emphasizes the Orthodox

---

[9] L. Zander, "Intercommunion and Co-celebration," in *Intercommunion*, pp. 351-60.

conception of the bloodless sacrifice and of the participation of all the saints in it. In the second objection Florovsky, without going into detail, includes "deep divergencies in doctrine in general," but he adds that "these divergencies, in our age at least, definitely cut across the historical confessions." His third objection refers to the doctrine of the ministry of the church. "A 'Catholic' cannot divorce order from faith; a very definite church order is for him an article of his integral Christian faith or dogma." He thus emphasizes that the point is not merely the restoration of an episcopal order, but the recognition of the sacramental character of the priesthood.

Florovsky has, no doubt intentionally, emphasized the rigid position of the Orthodox church. In some ways we may feel relieved that Rome is not the only church that candidly and freely declares itself "the only true Church." At the same time it cannot be denied that Florovsky's perhaps somewhat ironic description of the "Protestant" self-consciousness presents some serious questions to the churches of the Reformation. We shall return later to these questions.

It is not strange that Florovsky from his point of view should characterize the ecumenical movement as "a venture or an adventure." Certainly it is that, from every point of view. It may seem more surprising that he describes the movement as "a fellowship in search." When we are told that the way to "reunion" is by conversion to Orthodoxy, we are certainly tempted to assume that "search" has reference only to the "Protestants" and that "fellowship" is nonexistent. This interpretation seems to be confirmed when in the last words of the article Florovsky states his reasons for the participation of Orthodox theologians in ecumenical deliberations. There is, he says, "a certain rule of faith and order that is to be regarded as normal. What is beyond is just abnormal. But the abnormal should be cured, and not simply condemned. This is a justification for the participation of an Orthodox in the ecumenical discourse, in the hope that through his witness the Truth of God may win human hearts and minds."

In spite of this candidly emphasized missionary aspect it would be wrong to consider "fellowship in search" as only idle words. That does not represent Florovsky's view at all. On the contrary, the fellowship exists in spite of all divergences. The meaning of the ecumenical movement is that all Christians should pledge themselves to stay together, to profess their common allegiance to the same Lord, and to bear with patience the cross of division. "Tension remains, compelling us to move on." It is true that some unexpected agreements have been discovered, but "there is still a long and dangerous way ahead." We must also observe in this connection that the Orthodox church is not considered "perfect." Furthermore, in spite of all its rigidity Orthodoxy is characterized by a remarkable elasticity which is far different from an inflexible legalism and institutionalism. Such an elasticity has been manifested in various ways and in different degrees by nearly all the Orthodox theologians who have expressed themselves on ecumenical questions. It is to be found in statements about doctrine—the tradition—and the constitution of the church.

Orthodox theologians emphatically declare that they possess the true tradition of doctrine as it has been shaped and fixed by Scripture and the living tradition of the church. To them the relationship between Scripture and tradition is not a problem. They find it rather self-evident that there exists full harmony between them. Tradition has its basis in the Scriptures, but Scripture is interpreted through the tradition which flourishes in the church under the guidance of the Holy Spirit. They also underscore the importance of the ecumenical councils.

This conception does not mean, however, that they are strictly committed to the once-for-all established formulas, or to the idea that the living tradition ceased operating after the last council. Nicolas Zernov claims, for instance, that theories which have maintained the definitive authority of the old ecumenical councils belong to the periods of the church's weakness and are not typical of the Orthodox point of view. The East does not see the question of authority in the same light as the West. In contrast to the Western churches the Eastern church will not commit supreme authority to any documents, governmental office, councils, or to the Pope, or to any agency through which doctrinal authority would become legally defined. The Orthodox church

11

points rather to the Holy Spirit who speak and acts through the whole communion of saints. Zernov refers to a statement by Florovsky: "Tradition is the witness of the Holy Spirit, His unceasing revelation and preaching of Good Tidings. For the living members of the Church it is not an outward historical authority but the eternal continual voice of God, not only the voice of the past, but the voice of eternity." [10]

It is evident, therefore, that tradition is not definitely confined to formulas fixed in the past. To be sure, the old councils have an authoritative position. But however strongly this may be emphasized, nothing prevents a re-examination of the pronouncements of history, and in every case these pronouncements must be interpreted "historically and spiritually." Such utterances indicate a certain elasticity, which nevertheless is connected with an assured stability in reference to the ancient heritage. To create new dogmas, as Rome does, or new confessions, as the "Protestant" churches have done, is completely foreign to the Orthodox church. The chief confession is the Nicene Creed, further elaborated in the Chalcedonian formula and inseparably connected with the liturgy. The christological dogma of the ancient church is undoubtedly the principal dogma of the Eastern Orthodox church.

The view of the church as explicated by the Orthodox theologians has a character *sui generis*. The institutional element is impressively emphasized. But however strongly the importance of the firm organization of the church and of the episcopal order may be accentuated, the primary outlook is not institutional. The primary factor is the church as a communion, or, using the frequently recurring Russian expression, *sobornost*. In relation to *communio* all organization is secondary. Orthodox theology is aware of having preserved the connection with the ancient church and the church fathers, but also and foremost with the New Testament. It is also aware of being clearly differentiated from the more or less institutional conception of the church which characterizes the development of the medieval Roman church.

Orthodox theologians can speak of the church as an "organism," but according to Florovsky this cannot be done without

[10] Nicolas Zernov, *Den ortodoxa kyrkan* (1955), pp. 35ff.

12

certain restrictions. The idea of an organism has its own limitations. The church is composed of human personalities, which can never be regarded simply as cells of the whole. The personal is not to be sacrificed or dissolved in the corporate Christian "togetherness." "The idea of the organism must be supplemented by the idea of a symphony of personalities, in which the mystery of the Holy Trinity is reflected. This is the core of the conception of 'catholicity' (*sobornost*). This is the chief reason why we should prefer a christological orientation in the theology of the Church rather than a pneumatological." The church as a whole has its personal center only in Christ. She is "not an incarnation of the Holy Spirit, nor is she merely a Spirit-bearing community, but precisely the Body of Christ, the incarnate Lord." [11] Similar points of view are explicated by Bishop Cassian in an article, "The Family of God," published in *The Ecumenical Review*.[12]

If the church is defined primarily as communion, *sobornost*, attention is directed first of all towards the local congregations, not to the great "autocephalous" churches. These congregations represent the fundamental unity of the church, and, according to Orthodox theologians, this unity has its source in the Eucharist. It has therefore a sacramental character. Because the conception of the church is so thoroughly dominated by the sacramental perspective, it is necessary to discover what significance is given to "sacramental" in this connection. According to Florovsky, "sacramental means no less than *eschatological*." "*To eschaton* does not mean primarily *final*, in the temporal series of events; it means rather *ultimate* (decisive); and the ultimate is being realized within the stress of historical happenings and events. What is 'not of the world' is here 'in this world,' giving to it a new value, 'transvaluating' the world, as it were. Surely there is still only an anticipation, a 'token' of a final consummation. Yet the Spirit abides in the Church. This constitutes the mystery of the Church: a visible 'society' of frail men *is* an organism of the Divine Grace." [13]

[11] G. Florovsky, "The Church, Her Nature and Task," in *Man's Disorder and God's Design* (New York: Harper, 1949), pp. 53ff.
[12] *The Ecumenical Review*, 1957, pp. 129-42.
[13] Florovsky, "The Church, her Nature and Task," in *Man's Disorder and God's Design*, p. 54.

The unity of the church existing in the local congregations expands through the episcopacy to a universal unity. "Pentecost is continued and made permanent in the Church by means of the Apostolic Succession." But in this respect, too, we find that the idea of church-*communio* is considered primary in relation to the organization. "The Apostolic Succession is not so much the canonical as the mystical foundation of Church unity." [14] The most important thing is not a centralized organization. The unity of the Eastern Orthodox church, it is said, has been maintained without a centralized authority such as the Pope. "The East has, in fact, maintained its loose unity more successfully than the West: though, like the West, it has sometimes broken it by holding it too tight, as in the schism of the Russian Old-Believers. The Orthodox have been supported through all their trials by their conviction that so long as concord and charity are preserved the Church has nothing to fear." [15]

We have listened to Florovsky speak about the Orthodox church as the only true one, and at the same time we have heard him deny that it is "perfect." The church, he says, is at the same time the church of the redeemed and of poor sinners. This theme is repeated frequently in the pronouncements of Orthodox theologians. Antoine Kartachoff maintains that to regard anything in the church as absolute and to eliminate everything relative and human is *de facto* to fall into the Monophysite heresy. "It is high time that we gave up using the divine nature of the Church to cover up the sins and defects of Church life." "The Church has a kernel of infallibility and a foundation which is impeccable, but certain aspects of it are subject to sin." "The Church must realize that it is diphysite (dual in nature)." "It must have the courage to recognize its sins in history, its human weaknesses, the errors in its life and work, and must make an effort to correct them." [16]

Before leaving the Orthodox church we must add that the missionary aspect accentuated by Florovsky is not the only one raised by him or by other Orthodox theologians. Kartachoff tells

[14] *Ibid.*, pp. 50-51.
[15] Zernov, *op. cit.*, pp. 92-93.
[16] Antoine Kartachoff, "Orthodox Theology and the Ecumenical Movement," in *The Ecumenical Review*, 1955, pp. 32-33.

us, for instance, that "as a whole the Orthodox Institute of Theology in Paris, as an institution under the supreme protection of the Ecumenical Patriarch, welcomes the ecumenical collaboration of the Christian Churches as a blessed gift bestowed upon the Christians of our time." [17] The Metropolitan James of Melita speaks about the ecumenical work as a challenge to the old churches and concludes with the following words: "The older Churches can therefore glorify the name of the Lord in that He has given them the World Council of Churches, a council rekindling faith in God, charity among men and hope for a new understanding and unity." [18] The well-known Greek theologian, Hamilcar Alivasatos, a faithful participant in ecumenical deliberations, is very outspoken in regard to obstacles and difficulties. But in spite of this fact he is "full of hope in a wholehearted co-operation of the Orthodox Church with other Churches in the future. So much has come from the present limited co-operation, that when political conditions make possible a full co-operation of the Orthodox Church as a whole, the effect cannot be imagined." [19]

3. THE CHURCH OF ROME

The Roman church has not participated in the ecumenical deliberations by sending delegates, but we have very good reasons for saying that Rome has always been invisibly present. The participants in the discussions have never been able to ignore the fact that the largest of the Christian communions has remained outside. The very word ecumenicity is a constant reminder that the goal cannot be to manifest a Christian fellowship alongside of Rome, and still less in opposition to it.

However, we are interested now not in what attitude the ecumenical movement has taken toward Rome, but in how Rome has reacted to these efforts. We must first say a few words about the attitude of the Vatican as this has been expressed in the papal documents, *Mortalium animos* (1928), *Monitum* (1948),

[17] *Ibid.*, p. 35.
[18] James of Melita, "The Significance of the World Council of Churches for the Older Churches," in *The Ecumenical Review,* 1956, p. 18.
[19] Hamilcar Alivasatos, "Orthodoxy, Protestantism and the World Council of Churches," in *The Ecumenical Review,* 1954, pp. 277-86.

and *Instructio* (1949). In all three of these writings the Pope declares his great interest in the cause of unity. The encyclical *Mortalium animos* asserts, however, that no unity can be realized except on the basis of the return of straying Christians to Rome. With specific reference to the Conference in Amsterdam a restraining order was issued in *Monitum* restraining Roman laymen and priests from official participation with non-Catholics in conversations about religious questions without specific permission from the Holy See. This prohibition was directed especially toward ecumenical conferences. In *Instructio* we discern a somewhat modified tone. There is certainly no change in regard to the realization of unity. But it is noticeable that the document not only says that Rome observes the present struggle for unity with profound interest, but also very cautiously grants a certain recognition to what is now taking place. The growing desire for the realization of unity, it is said, bears witness to the gracious influence of the Spirit.

What the Vatican says about following new trends within non-Roman communions with lively interest is fully substantiated by the activity of Roman theologians. With the obvious approval of the hierarchy Roman theologians have commented extensively on ecumenical discussions and documents, especially in publications of their own church. It is gratifying to find that nothing has hindered Roman theologians from having their contributions published in the ecumenical movement's own organ, *The Ecumenical Review*, as well as in some of the studies prepared for ecumenical conferences. A number of presentations about the ecumenical movement from Rome's point of view have been published.[20]

What we have said thus far indicates that Rome looks upon the modern ecumenical struggle as a movement of great importance in the history of the church. When Rome maintains that no unity is possible except on the basis of a reunion with the Roman church, it is true to its own characteristic conception of the church. But this general position does not mean that Rome maintains an undifferentiated and identical attitude toward

[20] Gustaf Wingren, "Ekumenik och teologi," in *Studier tillägnade Hjalmar Lindroth* (Stockholm, 1958). Hereafter referred to as *Studier*.

the different non-Roman communions. There is an obvious difference between Rome's relationship to the Orthodox church and
that to the churches of the Reformation. In concentrating our
attention on the position Rome assumes at the present time with
regard to the Reformation, we now touch on a problem which to
a very high degree has interested contemporary Roman theologians, and which they have dealt with in a way quite different
from that of the older, traditional treatment.

Much has happened in the church of Rome during the last
hundred years. It would be a grave mistake to assume that this
church remains unchanged forever. On the contrary, it is characterized by a very lively development. The question as to
whether this development involves an approach to or a further
separation from evangelical churches and theology is extremely
complicated and cannot be answered by a simple yes or no. The
dominant impression we receive is that in general it has been
marked by different and contrary tendencies. On the one hand,
we can point to the continuing Roman development of dogma.
It is obvious that such new dogmas as papal infallibility (1870),
and the two Marian dogmas of 1854 and 1950 have widened the
distance between Rome and evangelical Christendom. On the
other hand, however, we find a number of factors in Roman
church life and theology which is any case give promise of making new contacts possible between them. In this connection we
may point to the modern Roman biblical studies, which are
pursued intensively; to the growing interest in the liturgy and
theology of the ancient church; and not least to the movements
for liturgical reform which have appeared in various places, especially in German and French Roman Catholicism. Much has
been written about these matters. One of the most significant
and, it seems, most influential works is the comprehensive interpretation of the meaning of the struggle for reform by the
French theologian Yves Congar in his book, *Vraie et fausse réforme dans l'église* (1950). Another French author, Louis
Bouyer, professor in *L'Institut Catholique* in Paris, has discussed
liturgical questions with frank criticism of the development within
the Roman church from the Middle Ages to the present. This
has appeared in English as *Liturgical Piety*.

When we examine what Roman theologians have written about the Reformation and Luther during the last twenty years, it appears very clearly that their work involves a rather thorough reconsideration of Rome's traditional attitude.[21] The pioneering works leading to a modified and more positive view of Luther have been such books as *Die Reformation in Deutschland* (1939-40), by Joseph Lortz, and *Luther in katholischer Sicht* (1947), by Johannes Hessen. It was of great importance that Adolf Herte in a three-volume work with the title, *Das katholische Lutherbild im Bann der Lutherkommentare des Cochläus* (1943), demonstrated in detail how the Roman interpretations of Luther had for centuries been dependent upon and determined by the purely abusive work published by Cochläus in 1549, *Commentarii de actis et scriptis Martini Lutheri*. Through these and other writings Roman theologians have begun more and more to emphasize the positive, religious motives in Luther's Reformation struggle. We might also emphasize that the Reformation, not only in its own time but even now, poses questions to which Rome and its theologians ought to pay close attention. All this means that the discussion has entered a new phase. It means especially that the appraisement of the Reformation is no longer as stereotyped as it has traditionally been. The traditional attitude has of course been matched from the evangelical side by a similarly stereotyped estimate of Rome.

But these changes within Roman theology do not mean at all that criticism of the Reformation is on the point of disappearing. To some extent, as we shall see below, criticism has shifted to areas other than those formerly in question. But it has not lost anything of its severity. Louis Bouyer, mentioned above, published in 1954 a book with the title, *Du protestantisme à l'Église* —a title which indicates that this author, a convert to Rome, wants to show others the way he himself has traveled. The English translation (1955) has a more neutral title: *The Spirit and Forms of Protestantism*. G. de Broglie, S.J., has written a com-

---

[21] Cf. K. E. Skydsgaard, *One in Christ* (Philadelphia: Muhlenberg, 1957); P. E. Persson, "Reformationen i nyare katolsk teologi," in *Svensk Teologisk Kvartalskrift* (1957); Walter Von Loewenich, *Der moderne Katholizismus* (1955).

mending preface to this edition in which he expresses the opinion
that the first part of the work, which deals with the positive
factors in the Reformation, will come as a surprise to many
Roman Catholics. But, he continues, the later chapters will af-
front many Protestants, "disappointed that a work so promising
in the beginning should conclude on a note of severe criticism."
It need hardly be pointed out that the other books mentioned
here are also severely critical. In Congar's great work on true
and false reform we find a penetrating and theologically motivated
criticism. We may also point to another study by the same author,
"Regards et réflections sur la christologie de Luther." [22]

After this general orientation we proceed to a closer examination of what modern Roman theology has to say about the Reformation, negatively and positively, especially as it concerns Luther.
The fundamental point of view developed with many different
variations may be described as follows: Roman theologians give
full recognition to the positive intention inherent in the Reformation. This is true in respect to the formulas *sola gratia* and *sola
fide,* as well as to the strong emphasis on Scripture and its
authority. But the positive factors in the Reformation were combined with a number of negative ones which led to schism and
heresy. What the Reformation had to say positively was entirely
justified in an age characterized by "so advanced a state of religious and moral decay as was the Christian community at the
end of the Middle Ages." [23] This positive element in the Reformation was in essential agreement with "the best catholic
tradition." The negations were to a very large extent due to the
influence of the theology of the decadent nominalism in the later
part of the Middle Ages.

The Reformation slogan, "justification through faith alone,"
says Bouyer, expresses in reality that which is essential in regard
to salvation. Here we are really confronted with the following
alternative: "either we are *not* saved by divine grace, acknowl-
edged and accepted by faith, *or* this grace, which is in God, is

[22] In the large, composite work, *Das Konzil von Chalcedon*, III.
[23] Louis Bouyer, *The Spirit and Forms of Protestantism*, trans. A. V.
Littledale (London: Newman, 1956), p. 113. Hereafter referred to as
Spirit.

the sole cause of our salvation, and faith, which is in us, the sole means of access to it. For if there is something needed which has a source other than grace received by faith, we are confronted again with the impossible task of the salvation of man by man." [24] That this fundamental doctrine of the Reformation stands in complete agreement with what the Roman church teaches, Bouyer attempts to prove first on the basis of what was said against Pelagian ideas by the Council of Orange in A.D. 529, and then by reference to Thomas Aquinas and to certain pronouncements by the Council of Trent. Whether these references are conclusive or not we cannot discuss in this connection. What is most interesting is Bouyer's own thesis that what is usually called the fundamental principle of the Reformation, or to use Bouyer's own words, Luther's "basic intuition," is quite in line with "Catholic tradition" and can easily be incorporated into it. If both "Protestants" and "Catholics" could become convinced of this, the result would be that the chief cause of conflict between them would cease to exist. [25]

The distinction Bouyer makes here between the original intention of the Reformation and its later negatively determined development appears also in other contexts. Thus in commenting on Luther's "admirable commentary" on the second article of the Creed in the *Small Catechism* Bouyer maintains that the purely personal relationship between Christ and the Christian, expressed here and elsewhere, in itself signified a healthy reaction against the legalism and formalism present in contemporary church life. [26] The explanation of the second article, he says, is "the real heart of Lutheranism." Here, in contrast to later negative development, we meet a "positive" not a destructive individualism, an essentially pure expression of that kind of individualism which we meet in the great prophets, in Christ himself, and in "all the most orthodox among the great spiritual writers." [27]

When Bouyer deals with Luther's exegesis of Galatians 3:13 in the *Large Commentary on Galatians,* he fully acknowledges

[24] *Ibid.,* pp. 12-13, italics by Aulén.
[25] *Ibid.,* pp. 43-44.
[26] *Ibid.,* pp. 100-01.
[27] *Ibid.,* p. 109.

the breadth and the depth of Luther's conception of salvation. His conception is not limited to the individual's forgiveness of sins. It is a comprehensive conception which transcends the moralism of both the "protagonists" of the Reformation and their "Catholic contemporaries." It also "transcends individualism, since it makes of grace, not an abstract concept, but a vital intuition of the person of Christ, vanquishing all by the power of the Cross, and drawing us by his resurrection into his kingdom." The description of the redemptive work of Christ in the Commentary on Galatians shows "what a force for the renewal of apostolic Christianity, in its traditional and patristic exposition, the Lutheran insight could have been, has been, and, in fact, remains, within the best type of Protestantism." [28]

What is true of the principle "justification by grace through faith" is true also of "the second Protestant principle," the supreme authority of the Bible. This, too, was "a return to the essential." Scripture indeed, as far as the learned were concerned, had "disappeared in the medley of decadent scholasticism," and, for the "unlettered," it had given "place to legends and popular devotions far removed from revealed doctrine." [29] This attitude of the Reformation was nothing else than a return to sound Catholic doctrine. It is true that later Catholicism has emphasized that the tradition is indispensable for the interpretation of Scripture. But it has not done so in order to bestow a higher degree of authority to the church than to Scripture, or in general to strengthen the authority of the church at the expense of Scripture. The doctrinal authority of the church, its *magisterium*, is necessary to insure both our own and the church's obedience to Scripture. Bouyer points out that according to both the Council of Trent and *Vaticanum* Scripture *alone* can be said to have God as its author. He concedes that the reaction to the Reformation as directed by the Council of Trent produced a certain restrained attitude toward the Bible, but he insists that this has been overcome in modern Catholicism, which strongly asserts that the Bible is the source of all theology and of spiritual

[28] *Ibid.*, pp. 57-58.
[29] *Ibid.*, pp. 14-15.

life, and which also therefore is vitally interested in the distribution and study of the Bible.

We have shown that the recognition which may be given to the "positive" aspects of the Reformation is combined with criticism against certain factors in the history of the Roman church. The writers are critical of the general conditions of the church at the time of the Reformation, of the decadent Scholasticism of the immediately preceding period, and also of the factually inadequate way the defense against the Reformation attack was conducted by contemporary Roman theologians.[30] For our understanding of the changes in the attitude of Roman theology to the Reformation and its message it is just as instructive to pay attention to this kind of critical self-examination as to the positive statements referred to above. In this connection, therefore, it is pertinent to investigate briefly that critical self-examination which expresses itself in the modern liturgical reform movements within the Roman church. What I have said here does not imply at all that this internal Roman criticism simply by itself would involve an approach to Reformation points of view. Such an interpretation would be completely contrary to the intention of the theologians quoted. Their position is clearly expressed in the title of Congar's great work: the purpose is to distinguish between the legitimate, necessary, and "true" reformation in contrast to the "false" Reformation of the sixteenth century. However this may be, it is clear that new contacts may be established to the extent that the reform movement ties in with the ancient church and the church fathers—not to mention also the Bible.

The two books by Congar and Bouyer provide excellent information about the meaning of the struggle for reform. Congar develops the fundamental principles, and Bouyer's book on the liturgy presents a thoroughgoing analysis of the departures of the liturgical development from what was original and essential. His book could be characterized as a study of true and false liturgy.

Congar differentiates between three different kinds of reform

[30] Thus for example, E. Iserloh, *Der Kampf um die Messe in ersten Jahren der Auseinandersetzung mit Luther* (1952).

efforts. In the first place efforts may be directed toward the elimination of certain abuses. In the second place they may be concerned with a reformation of doctrine, as the Protestants were. The reformation which Congar advocates, however, is intended to go deeper than simply an elimination of abuses, but he does not intend to direct the criticism against the "doctrinal, sacramental and hierarchical" structure of the church.[31] He does not seek the solution apart from or in opposition to the tradition of the church, but rather in that which most essentially characterizes this tradition (*dans la profondeur même de cette tradition*).[32] In contrast to the heretical movements the primary concern is not "a critical and constructive démarche," but rather "a submission to the Christian reality given in the Church." Reform efforts like these are characterized by pastoral interests. This attitude does not exclude considerable latitude and freedom.[33] But activity is carried on *"within* the Church and in agreement with its spirit"—and in order to serve the church.

When we review Bouyer's presentation of the liturgical development within the Roman church, we discover that in reality he considers the whole development from the thirteenth century on as a departure from a liturgy[34] in spirit and in truth. To be sure, Romanticism involved a reaction against the profane spirit that characterized the baroque period. But Romanticism did not produce a real renewal either. A real renewal has become possible only because in the present century attention has been directed toward "the patristic, liturgical heritage."

The Franciscans of the thirteenth century established the type of piety that emphasizes purely human emotions in the presence of the humanity of Christ. The cult of the child in the manger and the mysticism of the stigmata were typical expressions of this new spirituality. The Rosary and the reading of *Pater noster*

[31] Yves Congar, *Vraie et fausse réforme dans l'Église* (Paris, 1950), p. 186. Hereafter referred to as Congar, *Vraie.*

[32] *Ibid.,* p. 59.

[33] *Ibid.,* p. 250.

[34] Louis Bouyer defines liturgy as "that system of prayers and rites traditionally canonized by the Church as her own prayer and worship" (*Liturgical Piety* ["Notre Dame University Liturgical Studies," Vol. I] [Notre Dame, Ind.: Univ. of Notre Dame Pr., 1955], p. 1. Hereafter referred to as *Piety).*

and *Ave Maria,* which were given to the laity as a substitute for the Divine Office, "had the great merit of a primitive simplicity." They could lead to "a very pure contemplative, prayer" provided that proper instruction "in the Christian Mystery" had been given. "But the popular devotion to the Child Jesus, the Way of the Cross (following the stages of the Passion but with no reminder of the Resurrection), and, later on, the devotion to the Blessed Sacrament thought of as a kind of substitute for our Lord's sensible presence during the days of His earthly life,—all these were certainly so many developments at least foreign to the spirit of the liturgy, and often unconsciously but all too easily adopted in complete opposition to it." When the presence of Christ in the Sacrament is conceived of in this way, and when in addition this sacramental piety was separated from the Mass and even from Communion, "this threatened to wipe out the whole idea of the sacramental order and of the presence of Christ *in mysterio.*"[35] New devotions of this kind were not only foreign to the liturgy but were almost irreconcilable with it. "You cannot combine a mysticism centered on Jesus considered as the 'Prisoner of the tabernacle,' with celebrating the Eucharist as the saving Mystery by which Christ sets us free from all created limitations to bring us into the divine life." "When the development of certain extra-liturgical devotions arises from the fact that the liturgy is dying, and arises from the very causes which are the death of the liturgy, we cannot hope to return to a living liturgy while we concentrate on these devotions and even add to them."

This sharp criticism seems to lead at once to a demand for the elimination of these objectionable devotions, but that is not at all Bouyer's meaning. He emphasizes again and again that as seen in their historical setting they are not to be condemned. If the people of that time, when the liturgy was taken away from them, had not had these devotions, "they would have had nothing at all, and they would have lost all Christianity." But whatever was gained was bought at too high a price. These forms of devotion, foreign to the true liturgy, produced a climate favorable to the growth of Protestantism. The Reformers reacted against

[35] *Ibid.,* pp. 245ff.

these extreme transformations of traditional piety. Bouyer maintains that their efforts did not lead to any true reformation because Protestantism itself is to a great extent the fruit of the seed found in Medieval piety: "a naturalistic outlook on religion, a systematic ignoring of the Mystery, a sentimental kind of religious 'experience' in place of the sober mysticism, completely grounded on faith, of the great Christian tradition."[36]

It would take us too far from the subject to record how Bouyer thinks a solution may be found for the problem of the "extra-liturgical" types of piety. His fundamental point of view is that they should not be suppressed, but that an attempt should be made to pour the true spirit of the tradition into them, even into those forms which seem to be farthest away from "the authentic tradition," and thus to incorporate them "into the main stream of life." What is most important in all liturgical reform is that the Mystery, which is the central content of the liturgy, may be fully expressed. The spirit of the liturgy, which is nothing else than the spirit of the tradition, must be restored. Only then can the liturgy be for modern man what it really is: the true source of life. But Bouyer emphasizes that we cannot "give back the liturgy to the people without at the same time giving them full and immediate access to the Bible." By meditation on the Bible "in the school of the liturgy itself" the Bible itself will be illuminated for us "by the reality of the Mystery;" and in this way "the danger of an approach to the Bible without or against the Church will be avoided." This theme—the inseparable connection between the Mystery, the Eucharist, and the Bible—is developed with great energy by the Italian theologian, Divo Barsotti, in his book, *Il mistero christiano e la parola di Dio.* This work, which is typical of the "Bible renaissance," speaks of "the Word" as a means of grace in a way that is closely related to what is usually said in the churches of the Reformation. We will return later to Barsotti's very interesting presentation.[37]

We proceed now to a more detailed discussion of the criticisms that have been leveled against the Reformation. If we confine

[36] *Ibid.,* p. 249.
[37] Divo Barsotti, *Il mistero christiano e la parola di Dio* (1953). See below pp. 123-24.

ourselves to the books published within the last decade, we may start with the great work of Yves Congar. The critical remarks Congar makes have in many respects a close affinity with those made earlier by authors who have been relatively appreciative of the Reformation. He is in close agreement with Lortz, who maintains that Luther's position is characterized by a one-sided Paulinism and subjectivism. He regards Luther's alleged "objectivism" in his struggle against "the sectaries" as a temporary deviation. A real "objectivism," says Lortz, means that a person submits to the authority of the church and to its *magisterium*. Both Congar and Lortz agree in claiming that the Reformation criticism does not affect genuine Catholicism, but strikes rather, as far as theology is concerned, at the nominalistic theology of Occam at the close of the Middle Ages, on which Luther himself was dependent. But even though there is a similarity between Lortz and Congar on these and other points, we must note that Congar has in various ways sought to provide a more profound basis for criticism of the Reformation. What is especially interesting in this connection is that he concentrates on a critical analysis of the attitude of the Reformation to the means of grace, and that he follows this up by positing a fundamental antithesis between Rome and the Reformation in regard to Christology. With these critical remarks as a starting point Congar wants to emphasize and provide a broader basis for Rome's traditional objections to Luther's "spiritual" conception of the church.

Since Congar wants to base the antithesis between Rome and the Reformation on a divergence in Christology, it may be proper to start with his conception of the christological difference. The difference, he says, is concerned with the meaning of the Incarnation and its relationship to salvation. By way of introduction he emphasizes that the Christology of the Reformation is altogether soteriologically rather than ontologically oriented. The Incarnation meant that Christ took our sin upon himself, and justification meant that there was an exchange (*admirabile commercium*) between our sin which Christ assumed and his righteousness of which we become partakers (*iustitia extranea*). The difference between Rome and the Reformation is not that Rome talks about justification by works (Rome does not do that), nor that Luther excluded good works from the Christian life (he did not do so). The difference lies rather in the Reformation conception of salvation as exclusively a work of God. The consequence of this is that the divinity of Christ becomes the only meaningful christological reality. While Rome regards the humanity of Christ as "a holy humanity, a secondary but nevertheless real source of salvation," the Reformation assigns no real significance to it. The point is not ever that Christ co-operates with God. His humanity is the stage on which the redemptive drama takes place (*le théâtre de ce drame*). What happens in justification does not involve any real "communication" with Christ, but only that by faith his righteousness becomes ours. When Christ is said to be the Head of the church, the meaning is simply that Christ is the first man in whom the victory has been realized, and he is therefore the prototype of all men. "The humanity of Christ is where God's redemptive work first realizes itself. As man Christ does not do anything more than what we following him ought to do, viz., obey." Consequently, says Congar, Reformation Christology has in it "the taint of monophysitism, but he adds that it should rather be characterized as monergistic." [38]

Congar repeats again and again that the structure of Reformation Christology is soteriological rather than ontological and speculative. He notes, however, that this conception agrees more closely with "Semitic, prophetic and biblical rather than with Greek thinking" as found in the Christology of the ancient church.[39]

The defects which Congar believes he has found in the Christology of the Reformation have had serious effects on its conception of the means of grace and the church. The means of grace do not in any real sense become vehicles of grace. No matter how much Luther speaks of the "means of grace," of Baptism,

[38] Congar, "Regards et reflexions," p. 485. Cf. Sartory, *op. cit.,* p. 150.
de Luther," in *Das Konzil von Chalcedon* III, pp. 458-86. Cf. also Congar, *Vraie*, p. 402, and Sartory, *op. cit.,* p. 161. Sartory also speaks of the Reformation Christology as monophysitic. He also says, however, that the "genuinely Protestant" tendency to distinguish between the spiritual and the physical leads to Nestorianism (p. 168).
[39] Congar, "Regards et réflexions," p. 485. Cf. Sartory, *op. cit.,* p. 150.

the Eucharist, and the gospel, the decisive factor is nevertheless the fact that Christ deals with men "from above," "from heaven," through the Spirit. "Christ *alone* makes men Christian; alone, i.e., without the use of visible means." The means of grace are understood as "signs" rather than as effective means for the impartation of grace. The way in which the Reformers—Luther and Calvin—speak about "the Word" is, according to Congar, more congruent with the Old Testament than with the New, because "through and after the Incarnation God gives himself to us not only through his Word, but in reality and, as the fathers said in reference to the Spirit, substantially." What the Reformation said about "the Word" was to be sure both profound and true (*la grande part de vérité*), but it does not do justice to the reality of Christianity as a whole. [40] The incarnate Word does not deal with men directly from heaven in a spiritual manner; it deals with men in time. Through the church and the apostolic office there is a connection in time and space with the historical event of the cross. Luther's reference to the Word is in reality characterized by a dangerous ambiguity. He points indeed to something tangible, to the Bible and Christian preaching, but at the same time he speaks as if the Word were an independent and self-sufficient entity (*une réalité qui se pose par elle-même*). Congar refers to Karl Barth as a typical modern exponent of this ambiguity, but he holds that the same ambiguity was present also in Luther.[41]

It is clear that on the basis of this conception of the Reformation doctrine of the means of grace Congar must regard the Reformation view of the church as spiritualistic. Luther thinks of Christianity in terms of the Word and faith. The fundamental aspect of his view of the church is the antithesis between the external and the internal; the distinction between that which is external, bodily, and visible, and that which is Christian and spiritual. Congar calls this distinction "ruinous." From this point of view the true church becomes identified with the invisible church and with the fellowship (*communauté*) which is created through faith.

[40] Congar, *Vraie*, pp. 405-06.
[41] *Ibid.*, pp. 432-33.

The church becomes an assembly of believing people.[42] Luther is thus unable to understand how "an external form, a perceptible and bodily organism, can become a means of grace and by divine fiat something Christian and spiritual."[43] The church thus becomes merely something "inward," the spiritual fellowship constituted by the faith given by the Holy Spirit. Thus the idea of the church as precisely that body which in itself includes and fosters this fellowship is rejected.

Congar supposes (to be sure, not without cause) that "certain Lutherans" will react against this interpretation of Luther.[44] He is well aware that there are many statements of Luther that seem to point in an entirely different direction. At times he even attaches a slight reservation to his own interpretation. When he says that Luther was unable to conceive of the church as constituted by the activity of the means of grace, he adds in parenthesis after the word "not," "or not in any satisfactory way."[45] But he maintains that Luther's words about the effectiveness of the means of grace are in reality contrary to his fundamental conception (*l'dée profonde de Luther*). "In reality Luther's fundamental point of view, which in principle determines his actions, corrupts and destroys every affirmation of the visibility and substantiality of the true Church."[46] What Congar says in regard to Luther's well-known words about the church as the mother who bears and nurtures every Christian is typical. This "mothering," says Congar, does not really mean that the church bears us, but that it is "the place, the milieu, in which the Holy Spirit bears us through the Word and faith."[47]

The result of Congar's analysis is (as he says in a study called *Dogme christologique et Ecclesiologie*[48]) that the Reformation introduces a division between the church which is the object of faith and a result of God's act, and the empirical church which is the result of human activity. In contrast to this view Congar develops what he regards as decisive in the Roman theory of

[42] *Ibid.*, p. 458.
[43] *Ibid.*, p. 392.
[44] *Ibid.*, p. 408.
[45] *Ibid.*, p. 382.
[46] *Ibid.*, p. 410.
[47] *Ibid.*, p. 405.
[48] Congar, "Regards et réflexions," *op. cit.*, p. 245.

the church. The most interesting of these points are the following: the explication of the divine and human aspects of the church, the closely related problem of its holiness and sinfulness, the apostolic ministry, and the *magisterium* and tradition of the church.

As an agency of salvation and as an institution the church has "an immanent holiness" and "in a certain sense an infallibility, which comes from God alone, but which exists in *the Church,* in that Body of Christ which is at the same time visible and invisible, incarnate and spiritual."[49] This holiness and infallibility are related to the *structure* of the church. The trouble with the Reformers is that they fail to see how "the internal principles" of the church, or the visible body of the church, come from God. The failure to recognize this fact is contrary, not only to the tradition, but also to the New Testament. The primary factors involved are: 1) the fundamental deposit or content (*dépôt*) of faith, 2) the sacrament of faith, 3) the apostolic powers *(les pouvoirs apostoliques).*[50] The Protestants underrate that "guarantee" which has been given to the church through this threefold, God-given deposit, through the divine gift on which the sacraments and the ministerial functions depend, and through the Spirit residing in the church. In saying, therefore, that the church is infallible and irreformable the reference is to this fundamental and structural element *(ses éléments de fondation ou de structure).*[51]

But the concrete church is not only holy, it is also sinful. All its members are sinful with the exception of the blessed Virgin, who is also, as he says, "a symbol of the Church in its totality."[52] If we consider the church in "its concrete but adequate meaning," it is "at the same time holy and full of sin, unblemished and erring, perfect and laden with many historical imperfections." This ambiguity is due to its being at the same time divine and human.

In connection with his description of the church as at the same time infallible and erring Congar touches on the intricate

---

[49] Congar, *Vraie,* p. 456.
[50] *Ibid.,* p. 458.
[51] *Ibid.,* pp. 476ff.
[52] *Ibid.,* p. 107.

question about the infallibility which may be ascribed to the general *magisterium* of the church—particularly to the council of bishops—and to the Pope. Here, says Congar, we are dealing with an infallibility "under special conditions." It does not depend on "inspiration" but on an "assistance," which involves a guarantee of the decisions finally arrived at *(l'expression finale de travail)*. The history of the deliberations and decisions is frequently a very human history. The final decision, "the dogmatic definition," is divinely guaranteed against error, but the formulations are always historically conditioned and as such they cannot be made absolutely perfect.[53]

At this point we have already touched on "the apostolic ministry" and its functions. The Reformation conceives of the church only as a *communio sanctorum*. According to the "Catholic" view the church is both a *communio* and an apostolic institution. The church as *communio sanctorum* remains forever; it does not belong only to time. But when we consider how the church actualizes itself under the conditions of earthly life, the institutional church becomes primary in relation to the *communio*, just as the means precede the goal. In this connection the apostolic ministry has constitutive significance. The apostolic ministry functions in three different areas: as *magisterium* in regard to faith, in a sacerdotal capacity in reference to the sacraments, and as a pastoral government in respect to the life in the church.[54]

We are particularly interested here in what Congar has to say about the apostolic ministry as *magisterium*. What is its function in regard to the tradition and Scripture? Luther, says Congar, appealed to Scripture against the church and the Pope. Scripture and church are conceived of here as two "external" and opposing factors. When during the Reformation era "the Catholic apologists" objected to this conception, their defense, though in itself legitimate, was weakened because they did not fully analyze "the terms" they employed. The sad result was that their formulations seemed to accept the false schema of their opponents, viz., this opposition between Scripture and the church.

[53] *Ibid.*, p. 116.
[54] *Ibid.*, p. 413.

Congar finds the explanation of this in the fact that they were confined within a juridical and intellectualistic perspective, which in turn was derived from Medieval, ecclesiological formulations about power and authority of the church. If this question is to be correctly posed and actually solved, it must be taken out of the intellectualistic context and considered from a "realistic" point of view. "As reality the authority of the Church and the Pope does not come from Scripture but from the Lord who conferred it and has safeguarded its administration through his Spirit. Scripture bears witness to this reality, and it does so even if we were to regard it as only a historical document from which we can learn what Jesus had said, intended, and done." The church's true norm of faith is the tradition Christ gave to the apostles and which they transmitted to the church. In this connection Congar rejects as secondary the theory of the tradition as "the unwritten tradition," with which the Roman theologians of the sixteenth century operated in their polemics. Actually the tradition is the totality of "the realities" or of the means designed to awaken and sustain life in Christ: "the deposit of faith of which Scripture is a part, the sacraments, the powers of the ministry, the law of God, etc." [55] When the tradition is understood from this comprehensive point of view, the result is that Scripture and tradition cannot be thought of as two equal entities. Scripture is a part of the tradition, but it is the principal part. Holy Scripture, in conjunction with everything that has been given to mold the people of God under the new covenant, is the norm for the faith and life of the church and the principle that determines its structure. The church has received "this fundamental law" from Christ and the apostles. The episcopacy is the guardian of this law. But only the guardian. The *magisterium* of the church does not sit in judgment over Scripture; rather, it is judged by Scripture. But through its testimony the *magisterium* exercises its judgment over the interpretation of Scripture by the faithful.

In this connection Congar also discusses the part Scripture plays in efforts to reform the church. A true reform of the life of the church can take place only through a renewed contact with the principles of the church: its inner, spiritual principle

[55] *Ibid.*, pp. 487-88.

which is the Spirit of Christ, and its constitutive principle which consists of faith and the sacraments. A real and profound reform can come only "through a renewed consultation of the Church's fundamental tradition and of its 'monuments' among which Scripture is by far the most important." Congar says he is conscious of the fact that this position of Scripture within the framework of the tradition might seem not to do full justice to "the unique value of Scripture as the document of the will of God." He has been concerned to oppose "the error" in the Reformation doctrine of *sola scriptura.* We must take into account not only Scripture but the tradition as a whole. But *within this tradition* "Holy Scripture is the objective and regulatory norm." The biblical principle of the Reformation is not false, but it is inadequate, especially since it is not a matter only of "statements and ideas but of realities." [56]

One extremely serious question, according to Congar, is "the place of the doctors in the Church," or in other words, the position of scientific theological research. He points out the contrast to the Reformation. When the Reformation rejected the authority of the *magisterium,* the result was that the church was delivered to the *magisterium* of the "doctors," i.e., to the variable interpretations of Scripture by theological research. Besides, the church also became subject to secular authorities. Thus within Anglicanism Parliament and the Crown were given authority to make decisions even in matters of doctrine and worship. Luther on his part gave authority to "the princes" to institute reforms in regard to church discipline, but he denied their competence in regard to doctrine. But the princes exercised this right anyway in consultation with the theological faculties. It is not really surprising that Congar regards this problem as extremely serious even in reference to the Roman church. The problem is obvious. But Congar finds, however, that the general principle is clear. "The *magisterium* regulates the faith (*croyance*) of the faithful by virtue of its concern for and its *charisma* in reference to the apostolic witness. But the apostolic faith in the sense of a deposit of revealed truths determines the boundaries within which the

[56] *Ibid.,* pp. 491-99.

magisterium possesses authority and *charisma*." [57] The first statement emphasizes the inalienable prerogative of the hierarchy, the second defines the area within which the doctors can and should speak. The result of Congar's extensive deliberation and reasoning is that "scientific, theological, and historical research" is desirable from the point of view of the church, but the church is not without further consideration to listen to the latest conclusions of the critics. "The Church should follow and favor scientific research in order better to know and discern its true tradition."

Now that we have noted Congar's and Bouyer's fundamental points of view in regard to the Reformation, we must try to summarize their critical remarks. It is obvious that we meet here a much clearer comprehension of the intentions of the Reformation than has been found in older Roman polemical theology. We have also seen that they are as anxious as ever to establish the lines of demarcation between "Catholicism" and "Protestantism." It is no doubt true that, because these theologians are representatives of the liturgical reform movement, it becomes imperative for them to distinguish between "true" and "false" reform. Their definitions become especially interesting because we notice here certain shifts in emphases in contrast to the older formulations of controversial points.

We have seen that these Roman theologians manifest a rather generous appreciation of "the positive elements" in the Reformation. They acknowledge frankly that the situation in the Roman church at the time of the Reformation and during the later Middle Ages justified the striving for reform as this was expressed in the formulas *sola gratia* and *sola fide* and in the scriptural principle of the Reformation. Sartory declares that even "Luther's somewhat unfortunate formula, *simul iustus et peccator,* may be understood in a Catholic sense, provided it is not interpreted ontologically." [58] These Roman theologians admit both that during the later Middle Ages the Bible had been unduly neglected, and that the formulations of the Council of Trent unfortunately contributed for a long time toward a rather reserved attitude to the

[57] *Ibid.,* p. 523.
[58] Sartory, *op. cit.,* p. 201.

Scriptures. Several of the statements we have quoted from Congar and Bouyer indicate that they strive to give Scripture a stronger position than was possible as long as Scripture and tradition were considered of equal importance. We recall that, when Congar incorporates Scripture in the tradition, he maintains that Scripture is "the principal element." In this connection we may also refer to a dissertation by J. R. Geiselmann: "Das Konzil von Trent über das Verhältnis der heiligen Schrift und der nicht geschriebenen Tradition," with the subtitle, "Sein Missverständnis in der nachtridentinischen Theologie und die Überwindung dieses Missverständnisses." [59] This study endeavors to establish that, when the Council of Trent speaks of Scripture *and* tradition, according to the final formulation by the Council this "and" must not be interpreted as a reference partly to Scripture and partly to tradition (not: *partim—partim*). This interpretation nevertheless became the prevalent one down to the nineteenth century, but it has since been overcome especially through the work of the theologian J. E. Kuhn. To set Scripture and tradition side by side as equals is misleading. Holy Scripture mediates the gospel as the truth of revelation; the tradition mediates the gospel's revealed truth as exegesis and authoritative interpretation. This is the meaning of Congar's exposition of Scripture as the principal element of the tradition and of the authoritative interpretation by the *magisterium*. The criticism directed toward the scriptural principle of the Reformation is concerned, therefore, with its denial of the *magisterium* as authoritative interpreter.

The same criticism is directed toward those negations which they insist the Reformation has incorporated into the otherwise perfectly acceptable principle of *sola gratia, sola fide*. Bouyer insists that justification by faith means that man is merely "declared" righteous. Luther "unites two statements so closely that they become inseparable—one an affirmation, grace alone saves us; the second a negation, it changes nothing in us in so doing." [60] This is a one-sided interpretation of Paul, or, as Congar says, "a

[59] J. R. Geiselmann, "Das Konzil von Trent über das Verhältnis der heiligen Schrift und der nicht geschriebenen Tradition," in M. Schmaus (ed.), *Beiträge zum Begriff der Tradition*, pp. 125-206.
[60] Bouyer, *Spirit*, p. 139.

one-sided Galatianism." Such a pessimistic view is foreign to Paul and to the Bible in general.

This criticism of the Reformation doctrine of justification is connected with the oft-repeated criticism of its negative attitude toward the means of grace. The Reformation understands these as "signs," not as effectively working means of grace. Thus the Eucharist is reduced to a mere remembrance of the passion.[61] The Sacrament becomes a psychological stimulant for a wavering faith; a stimulant which a strong and robust faith does not need. Under such circumstances faith becomes not so much belief in an objective salvation, or in him who grants it, as faith in one's own individual salvation; in other words, faith is inclosed within itself.[62]

In a line of thought which frequently appears we find the assertion that *sola gratia* rightly derives salvation from God and understands it as his work, but that "Protestantism" disregards the means through which God works in history and in the church. This is the sense in which Congar interprets Anders Nygren's work, *Eros and Agape,* which he otherwise treasures very highly. Bouyer expresses the same idea more pointedly. He says that the Reformation correctly pointed to the fact that salvation is God's way to man and not man's way to God, but that at the same time it blocked God's way to man by its unsatisfactory view of the means of grace.

These critics of the Reformation go a step further when they point out that there is a contrast between Catholics and Protestants even in the conception of grace. The reason grace does not produce any real change in man is that grace is not conceived of ontologically and substantially. Even if Protestantism speaks of "a new creation," the reference is not to "an existential (*seinshafte*) change or an absorption of nature into supernature." The Reformation understands grace in terms of personal categories as God's favor and kindness. Roman theology, too, employs such "personal" terms, but grace means at the same time "a new, supernatural mode of existence." Both of these aspects may be combined. Ontological—personal may be *ein Gegensatz,* but it is *kein Widerspruch.*[63]

---

[61] Bouyer, *Piety,* p. 42.
[62] Bouyer, *Spirit,* pp. 140, 158.
[63] Sartory, *op. cit.,* pp. 109, 196-97.

We have seen that Congar tried to base the contrast between
Catholic and Protestant on a christological antithesis. His exposition of this subject is closely connected with what has been
said about the different conceptions of grace. The "ontological"
aspect is also found to be missing in the interpretation of the
Incarnation. Because this aspect is eliminated, the significance of
Christ's humanity is obscured. This is true in regard to its doctrines of both atonement and justification. Christ, who exists in
heaven, becomes isolated from the means of grace, and these
in turn are disqualified. Thus the Incarnation is not given proper
recognition. There is a gap between Christ and men. The idea
of a continuing incarnation refers, according to the Protestants,
to the invisible church, not to the visible. It is characteristic of
the Catholic conception, on the other hand, that Christ continues
his work through the visible church, through its ministry and sacraments. Protestantism justifies its rejection of this conception,
according to Sartory, by claiming that such a conception would
destroy the "uniqueness" (*Einmaligkeit*) of the person of Jesus
and endanger the "once-for-allness" (*Einzigkeit*) of his redemptive work. Behind this argument lies, as we have seen, the
opinion of the Roman theologians that the Christology of the
Reformation is one-sidedly soteriological, while the Christology
of the ancient church was overwhelmingly ontological. They also
claim that the Christology of the Reformation stands in conflict
with the decisions and formulas of the ecumenical councils, especially with Chalcedon.[64]

The above criticism of the Reformation has its focal point in
the severe criticism of its conception of the church, which we
have already sufficiently discussed. The spiritualistic and individualistic conception of the church, attributed to the Reformation,
is the result of its "negations" in regard to the doctrines of
Christology, the means of grace, and justification. In reality, however, the primary contrast would seem to be between the church
conceived of as invisible and spiritual, on the one hand, and the
church conceived of as visible and hierarchical, on the other hand.
This contrast is then explained by reference to the "negations."
At any rate, the contrast involved in the conception of the church

[64] *Ibid.*, pp. 150-51, 56, 70.

receives the greatest attention. Although in spite of everything the original antitheses have become somewhat less sharp—i.e., those which we usually refer to as the formal and material principles of the Reformation—the antithesis in regard to the conception of the church has become sharper. This is due especially to the development of the theories of "the hierarchical constitution of the church" during the past century, and above all to everything connected with the promulgation of the dogma of papal infallibility. It is evident that this dogma has sharpened the antagonism on the part of both the reformed communions and the Orthodox church. We will not enter into a discussion of this subject, but we might quote a few words Sartory has written about the primacy of the Pope, which are quite interesting. "The primacy as such rests on a divine institution, and sets forth a divine principle and a divine reality. The primacy of the Pope is a confessional truth which may be formulated thus: Christ has appointed Peter as the head of the college of apostles, and he has given this authority also to his successors. This is a mystery of faith. Here the distinction between the physical and the mystical person is exceedingly important. As physical persons the apostles have died and have been followed by other physical persons. As mystical persons 'the Twelve' abide in their successors. . . . This is true also of Peter. He does not cease to exist as the head. He abides in the Bishop of Rome. The popes, Linus, Cletus, Clement, and the rest of them are dead. Physically and spiritually they may have brought honor or shame to their See, they may have been saints or a Judas: this is of no importance whatever. Peter, the Head, in a mystical sense cannot die; he remains alive in them. This mystery is accessible only to the supernatural faith." [65]

Before we leave our review of the Roman theologians' treatment of the Reformation, we must note briefly the historical perspective they employ. Their fundamental point of view is clear. On the positive side there was really nothing new in the Reformation. Whatever of positive value the Reformation brought was good Catholic teaching, which indeed needed to be emphasized because during the later Middle Ages it had

[65] *Ibid.,* p. 157.

been more or less obscured in that period of both theological and liturgical decadence. It was the misfortune of the Reformation that it was dependent on these decadent movements and was thus betrayed into negative protests, which in reality had no essential connection with its positive program. But also the Roman apologetic of the sixteenth century was in its way dependent on the conditions created by the negations of the late Middle Ages and the Reformation, and consequently was not able to give an answer to the Reformation in accordance with the best Catholic tradition.

Here we are particularly interested in *how* the Reformation's dependence on the later Middle Ages is explained. In this connection Congar is able to refer to the spiritual reform movements which appeared now and again during the Middle Ages. But both he and Bouyer put the emphasis on Occamistic and nominalistic theology.[66] They point to the critical and radical empiricism of Occamism and to its dissolution of all general ideas, of the conception of substance and of metaphysics: a criticism which leads to the affirmation of the incomprehensibility of God. The attitude of nominalistic theology with respect to ecclesiology is especially significant. I quote here the general characterization given by Congar: "It involves a dissolution of the reliability of almost every statement about the structure of the Church, the function and powers of the hierarchy, a separation between the institutional and hierarchical church, which they despise, and the purely spiritual church which consists of true believers, a questioning of the present theology of the sacraments, and the inability, because of their voluntarism, to conceive of the Church as a sacramental organism." [67]

Bouyer shows how closely Luther is tied to nominalistic theology, and how this fact spoils whatever fruit may have come from Reformation efforts. Nominalism is the source of Luther's "negations." This is true, for example, of his interpretation of justification as a "declaration" of man's righteousness (extrinsic justification), of his subjective conception of faith, and also of his reference to God's Word over against the ecclesiastical institution.

[66] Congar, *Vraie*, pp. 372ff.; Bouyer, *Spirit*, pp. 153ff.
[67] *Ibid.*, p. 375.

But the Reformation is not only dependent on nominalistic theology; it is also, according to Bouyer, dependent on the decadent liturgical development during the later Middle Ages. He characterizes the eucharistic conception in Protestantism as "the idea of the Mass as an absorbing contemplation of Our Lord in His passion only, to the total exclusion of any thought of His Resurrection and of His final glory in His Whole Mystical Body, together with the reduction of the liturgical mystery to a mere memorial of His Passion—all this is nothing but the final development of the medieval over-emphasis on the suffering Humanity of Christ, combined with the effects of the gradual disappearance of the true idea of the liturgy as sacramental, this idea having already been buried under a merely sentimental and allegorical remembrance of the past." [68]

We may fittingly close this section on Rome and the Reformation by quoting one of the "conclusions" stated by Bouyer: "Our conclusion from this chapter is that the negative, 'heretical' aspect of the Reformation neither follows from its positive principles, nor is it a necessary consequence of their development or vindication, but appears simply as a survival, within Protestantism, of what was most vitiated and corrupt in the Catholic thought of the close of the Middle Ages." [69]

4. THE ANGLICAN CHURCH

The Reformation caused the deepest schism in the history of Christendom. The Lutheran, Reformed, and Anglican communions became separated from the Roman mother church. None of these churches regarded itself as "new." Any thoughts in that direction were completely foreign to them; in fact, such a conception was unthinkable. Each looked upon itself as a "reformed" continuation of the church of Christ, of the catholic and apostolic church.

Any attempt to characterize the genius of these communions associated with the Reformation and to delineate their mutual relationship lies entirely outside the scope of this book. Nor can we provide a review of their relationship to and their judg-

[68] Bouyer, *Piety,* p. 42.
[69] Bouyer, *Spirit,* p. 164.

ment of the Reformation during the course of history. Such a chapter would be of great interest in view of the changing aspects that have appeared from time to time. A few decades ago there appeared a book under the title, *Luther in den Wandlungen seiner* (!) *Kirche.* It contained a collection of the most divers portraits of Luther. Something similar could be said of the relationship of the Reformed church to Calvin; not to mention the very changeable attitude of the Anglican church to the Reformation.

As in this chapter we are reviewing the statements about the Reformation which have been made in connection with the ecumenical movement, the Anglican attitude calls for our special attention, not least because of the program which the Anglicans advocate in their ecumenical discussions. No other communion has made itself the spokesman for ecumenical endeavor as early and as energetically as the Anglicans. The immediate purpose of the deliberations this church has entered upon with other church bodies has been the establishment of church fellowship and communion. Such a church fellowship has generally been regarded as an intermediate point on the way to the final goal— the reunion of the churches. The action of the Anglican church has been supported by the conviction that it has special opportunities to mediate and build bridges between the "old" churches and the reformed communions, between "Catholic" and "Protestant." It holds that these opportunities are present because the Anglican church itself is characterized by a union of "Catholic" and reformed elements. This union, it is true, involves some very great tensions, but it has nevertheless demonstrated its ability to survive within the limits of the church. The "Catholic" element is represented by the strong emphasis on the connection with the ancient, undivided church, "the consensus of the first five centuries" (*consensus quinque-secularis*). But the most central element is above all "the historic episcopate." Whatever differences we may encounter within Anglicanism in this regard—and the differences are indeed great—the representatives of the Anglican church have always underscored the historic episcopate as founded on the apostolic succession.

One characteristic document is the article, "Anglicanism and Intercommunion," by one of the veterans among the Anglican ecumenical leaders, Professor Leonard Hodgson, published in the study volume, *Intercommunion*. The author is well aware that Anglican insistence on the historic episcopate as a prerequisite for intercommunion is apt to cause offense among other denominations. But this offense must not be taken as a reason for granting concessions which deny the fundamental point of view. The principle is unshakable. The idea held in some quarters that Anglicanism could easily be persuaded to abandon its position is contrary both to statements made by the leaders of the church and to the policy embodied in official acts. Such an abandonment would be disloyalty to the grace which has been given to the Anglican church and which makes it "possible for its members to live and worship together as sons both of the Reformation and of the historic Catholic Church." Neither Catholicism nor Protestantism "taken alone express the full truth of Christianity. We find it impossible to believe that the unity of Christendom will be achieved through either, so to speak, 'swallowing' the other." We regard "the apostolic succession as one of those valuable elements in the Catholic tradition which we treasure for ourselves and wish to share with others. . . . Any hopes of a united Christendom which is to include Anglicanism must include the hope that the rest of Christendom will welcome the opportunity of sharing in this treasure which has been given to the Anglican Church to be its contribution to the riches of the whole united body." [70]

Even if Hodgson intentionally overemphasizes the intransigence of the Anglicans, his statement nevertheless represents what may be called the official Anglicanism which regards the historic episcopate as essential for "organic reunion." But this does not mean that there is any uniform conception of the meaning and significance of the historic episcopate. In reality we meet a number of different interpretations. At this point we may examine a few of these different conceptions.

One type of interpretation emphasizes the value of the historic episcopate without assigning any dogmatic significance to it. Those who hold this view stress its significance from the point of view of historical continuity and claim that this provides a

[70] "Anglicanism and Intercommunion," in *Intercommunion*, pp. 255ff.

dimension of depth to the present office of the ministry. By rejecting the dogmatic aspect they escape the necessity of drawing any negative conclusions about the ministry and the administration of the means of grace in the churches that lack the historic episcopate. In this type of interpretation the historic episcopate may be regarded as belonging to "the fulness" of the church and is of its *bene esse* rather than its *esse*. In such connections we may come across the idea that a ministry without direct connection with the historic episcopate is valid within that particular communion, but that it would acquire a more universal character if it were incorporated within the framework of the historic episcopate. Another type of interpretation maintains that the historic episcopate as guaranteed by the apostolic succession belongs to the *esse* and being of the church. This involves certain dogmatic consequences. Those who hold this view must naturally show a more negative attitude toward the orders in those churches which lack the apostolic succession and the historic episcopate. But even among those who hold this view there are numerous variations, and the negative implications may be interpreted in different ways.

It is unnecessary to go into detail concerning the divergences in regard to the interpretation of the meaning and obligations of the historic episcopate. It is obvious that these divergences are related to different attitudes toward the Reformation. It is well known that the attitude varies a great deal, all the way from a wholehearted appreciation to the "Anglo-Catholic" faction's acknowledgment of the Reformation with very forceful reservations. As we shall see, the criticism is partly related to ideas we found in the works of the Roman theologians discussed in the previous chapter. This does not mean, however, that Anglo-Catholic criticism is directed solely toward "Protestantism"; Rome also receives its due share.

In this connection we are especially interested in what Anglo-Catholic theology has to say, positively and negatively, about the Reformation. Here we need not be concerned with a number of individual theologians. Our task is made a great deal easier because we are able to refer to an eminently representative document: a pamphlet entitled *Catholicity: A Study in the*

Conflict of Christian Traditions in the West.[71] This document, which is very carefully written, provides a clear and instructive account of the Anglo-Catholic position.

"In our divided Christendom we do not believe that any existing institution or group of institutions gives a full and balanced representation of the true and primitive Catholicity. It is the recovery of the principles of that Catholicity that is our quest." This introductory statement indicates how the Anglo-Catholic attitude differs from that of the Orthodox and the Roman. In a divided Christendom no denomination can claim exclusive possession of true "catholicity." It is asserted that this catholicity was lost long before the schism of the sixteenth century—in the separation between the East and the West. It cannot be regained by seeking to put the pieces together again, but must be attained through "a vital growth towards a genuine wholeness or catholicity of faith, thought and life." "Catholicity" is understood here in the sense of fulness or *wholeness*. It is the opposite of the fragmentation of faith, thought, and life which has broken Christendom into pieces.

In order to understand what they mean by "catholicity" it is necessary to understand how they conceive of original catholicity and "the primitive unity." This unity, it is said, "has sprung directly out of the entrance of God into human history in the eschatological event of Redemption." The church is a part of this eschatological redemption and of the gospel. Christ is at once the fulfilment of the old Israel and the head of the new Israel. The members do not constitute the church, but are rather brought into a unity which already exists. "The 'wholeness' manifests itself in this world in a visible Church." The paradoxical view of the church which we see in the apostolic writings maintains that the church is the Body of Christ, but that at the same time it is composed of sinful men. The true order is not: Christ—faithful individuals—the church, but Christ—the church —faithful individuals. "It is Christ-in-his-Body who justifies men, and their justification *is* their deliverance into His Body." The church manifests itself in its outward order. There is no sharp

[71] *Catholicity: A Study in the Conflict of Christian Traditions in the West* (London: Dacre, 1947).

44

distinction between the spiritual and the bodily. To receive the Spirit is to belong to the Body. In the outward order the apostles occupy a unique position because of the commission they received from the Lord and the authority to rule given to them. The "wholeness" embodies itself in Baptism and the Eucharist. Baptism incorporates the Christian into the people of God with all the privileges and the eternal goal involved in it. The Eucharist "expresses the intimate communion of the soul with its Lord and the corporate essence of the whole Church as the fruit of the Passion and Resurrection." The New Testament Scriptures proceed from this "Christian life, *lived* and embodied in dogma, worship and institutions." To put "Scripture" and "tradition" in opposition to one another is wholly artificial and arbitrary. "The apostolic 'writings' reflect and presuppose at every point the abundant many-sidedness and tension of the life of the Apostolic Church, and its 'tradition' of *kerygma* and practice." The canonization of Scripture provides an authoritative witness to and a norm for the preservation of this tradition. The authors of *Catholicity* arrive finally at this conclusion: "If theologians are not agreed from the outset in believing the Church to be a Divine fact prior to the individuals who compose its membership, in believing its outward order to be a part of its being, in affirming the unity of the faith, in recognizing the authority of 'Tradition' together with that of Scripture, then they have not reached agreement about the first principles of the unity they are seeking."

Catholicity, "wholeness," was lost in the separation between East and West. The Western church lived through the barbarian invasions and the succeeding "Dark Ages." When the time came for a reconstruction, the contact between Rome and the Eastern church had already been lost. What now appeared in the Western church was characterized by an administrative legalism resulting in clericalism, a new theological rationalism in the Scholastic systems, and, somewhat later, a new individualistic piety. In all these respects the Eastern church could have provided correctives if contact had been maintained. It was in close contact with social life, but without clericalism. It had retained the integrity of the faith, because it had never isolated the crucifixion as the West had done, but had rather emphasized that salvation was accomplished in the Incarnation, the cross, the resurrection, the ascension, the gift of the Spirit, and the second advent. It had also preserved the corporateness of worship and the participation of the church on earth in the communion of saints. The Eastern church, too, had suffered in various respects on account of the separation from the West, as, for instance, in its dependence on the state. It missed both the Renaissance and the Reformation, but as a compensation it preserved "the old traditions uncontaminated."

The authors of *Catholicity* intended to examine the Reformation in the light of this background. The Reformation was a reaction against "the defective tradition" within the Western church. As a result of this "defect" "the vital truths" of the Reformation could be proclaimed only in a fragmentary and one-sided way. Protestantism came with "great positive truths," but also with "radical errors."

We note first briefly what the authors have to say about the positive truths. There are five such truths. The first and most fundamental is "the gospel of the living God," which places God's direct and personal action in opposition to all "religion of works." In the person of Christ God has actively entered the world to save sinners and he continues this redemptive work now. The second truth has reference to the authority of the Bible as the primary and perfect witness to the saving work of God in Christ. Even if the interpretation was not always correct, nevertheless the appeal to the Bible has been the strength of Protestantism and has been of the greatest importance for Christendom as a whole. In the third place they point to the significance of the doctrine of justification by faith. Faith is personal response to the living God. "The essential point is that nothing can take the place of the *personal* response of man to God." A fourth important truth "was the active *participation of the laity* in the life and government of the church." Finally they underscore the significance of the fact that Protestantism "laid very great emphasis on the importance of *preaching*." The significance of this remains even though preaching "has not been seen in its right relation to Worship." This defect, according to the authors of *Catholicity,* is due to the one-sided emphasis on the doctrine of justification by faith *alone*. The assumption seems to be that this "alone" has resulted in obscuring the position of the Sacrament in worship.

We pass on now to critical statements about the Reformation. They have discovered two radical errors in Luther: first, that justification is dissociated from creation, and second, that justification is dissociated from sanctification.

In regard to the first point they maintain that the heavy emphasis on salvation by God's grace, which in itself is perfectly proper, is nevertheless secured at too high a price. Protestantism surrendered "the Biblical doctrine that man was made 'in the image of God,' and that this 'Image', though defaced by sin, substantially remains in fallen man, and is effectually restored by Baptism into Christ." They point to the "catastrophic pessimism" which characterizes Protestantism, and which leads to the conception that salvation is based on an arbitrary predestination on God's part, and they also note that the lost image is not effectively restored through "the imputed righteousness." The criticism is directed especially toward Luther's rejection of all "natural theology." Luther had discovered that natural theology had become unduly rationalistic in Medieval Scholasticism. When his attitude toward it became entirely negative, however, there were a number of dire consequences. The result was: 1) a distrust of philosophical thinking altogether; 2) an isolation of salvation from creation, of which both the Old and the New Testaments bear witness in the sense that salvation is conceived of as a renewal of the original creation through a second act of creation. Furthermore, Luther's position resulted in 3) "a loss, in large measure, of the sacramental principle which is involved in the Incarnation." One of the results of this was that Luther's very significant doctrine of Christian vocation became secularized because vocation was not conceived of in sacramental terms. Finally, 4) the conception of man's total depravity led to a retreat from history, because in the present the individual soul is confronted directly with Calvary as the only significant event in history—everything else is without importance.

The other error is concerned with the relationship between justification and sanctification. The truth the Reformation maintains may be expressed also in a statement like that of Nygren: "Our fellowship with God rests for us on the basis not of holiness but of sin." But, says *Catholicity,* "a truth that is expressed out of proportion with other truths sometimes becomes strangely changed into its opposite." This is the risk that accompanies the doctrine of justification by faith alone. When the attempt is made to maintain and preserve the experience of conversion without incorporating the faith-relationship into the sacramental framework, the result is a return to "subjectivism and the cultivation of religious feelings."

After this critical appraisal of the Reformation's "isolation" of justification, *Catholicity* proceeds to a critical analysis of the Reformation conception of the church and authority. There were good reasons for the criticism leveled by the Reformation. "The Middle Ages had blurred the distinction between the visible Church and the Kingdom of God, had neglected the theology of the Church as the Mystical Body of Christ, and had too often forgotten the dependence of the Church upon the Gospel of God. In different ways both Luther and Calvin sought to rediscover the roots of Biblical theology, from which the nature of the Church is derived; but in different ways they were blinded in their search by misleading presuppositions." Luther on his part maintains that the church, which is at the same time both visible and invisible, "is constituted by the presence of the means of grace." But something is lacking here. Luther has lost sight of the church's historical continuity with "the Word-made-Flesh." "The indifference of Lutheranism to the principle of succession in Church order is bound up with the loss of the conception of the Church as a continuous historical society, whose essence is, despite the imperfections of its members, the glorified Humanity of our Lord."

"Both Lutheranism and Calvinism imply a doctrine of the union of individual souls in the way of salvation prior to their incorporation into the visible Church." This conception results in the order which *Catholicity* has already declared to be misleading and contrary to the "catholic," i.e.: Christ—the individual Christian—the church.

From what we have said here it is obvious that there is a contrast between the Protestant and the Catholic conceptions of authority. In this case too it is easy to understand the violent opposition of the Reformation to a church in which the authority of the *magisterium* had too long been exercised without the necessary presuppositions, i.e., without the church itself embodying the apostolic tradition and being itself in subjection to the gospel of God. The Reformation sets up the authority of Scripture in opposition to the church, but the question must then be raised as to how Scripture is to be interpreted. It is not enough to appeal only to the "Bible" or to the "gospel." We cannot do this without at the same time appealing to the apostolic church as a witness to and preserver of both. This does not mean, to be sure, that an authority thus conceived of would be free from abuse within Catholicism. "Far from it. But the doctrine itself (about authority) is a part of apostolic Christianity, and its right exercise can only be recovered by a return to the fulness of the apostolic Tradition."

When *Catholicity* further on deals with modern ecumenical efforts, it decries the popular method of separating the question of "faith" from the question of "order." This sharp distinction, it is said, is the result of "a disintegrated theology and was unknown to the primitive Church. To build upon an antithesis between faith and order is therefore to promote not unity but further dissociation."

5. *POST-REFORMATION CHURCHES*

Since in this section we are dealing with the attitude of the various communions toward the Reformation, and giving special attention to criticisms leveled against it, we must also finally say a few words about those denominations that have originated since the Reformation. We will, however, bypass completely the conflicts between Lutherans and Reformed during and after the Reformation.

The separation between the churches at the time of the Reformation was followed by a number of later separations. The great majority of these—Baptists, Congregationists, Methodists—have come from the Reformed and the Anglican communions; in the case of the latter, especially from those areas subjected to Reformed influence. Nothing comparable has appeared within the Lutheran communion. The only significant exception is the small Moravian church. Though Lutheranism has thus proved to have a greater cohesiveness, the denominations originating in the Reformed tradition have demonstrated their ability to make inroads within Lutheran areas.

Post-Reformation denominations manifest a number of differences. Their attitude to the Reformation is also variable. The very fact that they broke away from the original churches of the Reformation indicates that they have also been opposed in some way to the Reformation. In reality their attitude to the Reformation must be characterized as ambiguous. On the one hand, the denominations in question have without doubt generally *desired* to maintain *sola gratia* in the spirit of the Reformation. They have also, most often in a very radical sense and with a complete rejection of all tradition, sought to uphold the Bible as the only norm for the life, teaching, order, and discipline of the church. We must note especially that, with an extreme accentuation of the traditional Reformed conception, they regard the biblical directions about organizational matters as binding for all time. The ideal would be a church order resembling as closely as possible the pattern of the primitive church.

This attitude is associated with a view of the church which is obviously opposed to that of the Reformation, and to both Luther and Calvin. This view of the church is found more or less clearly defined within all the post-Reformation denominations and constitutes one of their essential elements. It is characterized by the fact that faith and confession of faith are, at least in principle, the presupposition for membership in the church. Each particular communion must as far as possible consist of "pure" congregations. The desire is to establish visible boundaries around the communion of the faithful *(vere credentium et fidelium)*. This fundamental conception of the church may then be developed in various ways and be combined with different interpretations of perfectionism, the sacraments, the ministry, discipline, etc. But however the principle of faith as a prerequisite for membership may be further developed, it stands in obvious opposition to the conception of the church represented by the Reformation. *Here* we can say that the order is what *Catholicity* thought it found in the Reformation: Christ—the individual Christian believer—the church.

These various denominations are of course aware of the fact that the ideal of pure congregations can be only imperfectly realized. Even though this insight was not perfectly clear from the beginning, it has become more and more obvious. This means that they have entered upon a path which leads away from the exclusiveness which is and must be connected with the idea of a visible "pure" church. The wholehearted participation of the greater number of these post-Reformation denominations in the modern ecumenical movement bears witness to this fact. The ecumenical documents emanating from these sources claim instead that these denominations find it easier to establish connections beyond their boundaries than do the churches which are more closely tied to traditions. Several of the church mergers in modern times show that ecumenical conversations may lead not only across boundaries but also to their elimination. The most notable example is the Church of South India, which unites four types as structurally disparate as Congregational, Methodist, Presbyterian, and Anglican. We must note, however, that Anglicanism, as represented by the bishops of the various Anglican churches (the Lambeth Conference), have hitherto manifested a somewhat reserved attitude to the new church union and have not established full "communion" with it.

Especially interesting are the ecumenical documents emanating from the Baptist church. The Baptists in particular have emphasized faith and confession of faith as a condition for membership in the church by their rejection of infant baptism and their insistence on baptism as an act of confession which opens the door to membership in the church for the individual Christian. If this practice, according to the Baptist conception, is the only one that can be defended on biblical grounds, the result would seem to be a rejection of the churches which practice infant baptism.

The question is discussed by V. E. Devadutt in an article in *Intercommunion* with the title, "A Baptist View." There are, he says, two different groups among the Baptists: "the Strict

E   51

Baptists" and "the Open Baptists." The former would be very reluctant to recognize the Communion Service of any other Christian body but their own. They would also normally be adverse to admitting anyone to the Lord's Table who had not been baptized by immersion on the grounds of their profession of faith. The Strict Baptists, however, are a minority. "The Open Baptists, on the contrary, would welcome gladly to the Lord's Table anyone who 'loves the Lord Jesus Christ.' . . . They would also be ready to join with others at the Lord's Table, provided there is no insistence that in doing so they must subscribe to any specific interpretation of the Sacrament." [72] In another article with the same title, which deals with the situation in Britain, P. W. Evans declares that the development in the free churches toward "open communion" has spread to such an extent that the result has been "a mutual open communion," and they would gladly welcome Anglicans as well as free churchmen to the Lord's Table. [73]

A third Baptist author, R. Claibourne Johnson (U.S.A.), who discusses the Baptist point of view in *Ways of Worship,* speaks of baptism and the Eucharist as "ordinances." Baptism and the Lord's Supper are teaching ordinances, but they are not sacraments or vehicles of grace. Their value lies in their symbolizing the two truths which constitute the eternal gospel of grace, our Lord's death and resurrection. These ordinances "are accepted only by people whose experience of saving grace, which was made available by our Lord's death and resurrection, leads them to seek, in obedience to the Master's command, to proclaim their faith in the efficacy of His death and resurrection." Believers' baptism is a safeguard for a regenerate church membership. The practice of immersion was adopted because it symbolizes the death and resurrection of Christ. "Early Baptists, seeing the abuses that were in the Roman Church of their day, and even in the Reformation Churches of Luther and Calvin, owing to the inclusion of entire populations in the Church through the rite of infant baptism, were absolutely convinced that a regenerate membership could never be possible as long as this rite was prac-

[72] V. E. Devadutt, "A Baptist View," in *Intercommunion,* p. 178.
[73] P. W. Evans, "A Baptist View," in *Intercommunion,* pp. 185ff.

tised." In this connection Johnson points to the lively debate about infant baptism in recent times and especially to the statements by the two Swiss theologians, Brunner and Barth. "The contemporary practice of infant baptism, says Brunner, can hardly be regarded as being anything short of scandalous." Barth calls the practice of infant baptism "arbitrary and despotic." It can be established, says Johnson, "by exegesis and from the nature of the case, that in this rite the baptised person must be an active partner. . . . Plainly, says Barth, no infant can be such a person." [74]

We have noted Johnson's statement that the Baptists regard Baptism and the Lord's Supper as "ordinances," but not as vehicles of grace or means of grace. This conception, however, does not seem to be universally accepted. In the article previously quoted Devadutt says that "all Baptists would readily agree that the Lord's Supper is a memorial feast," but that "many would maintain that it is more than a mere formal memorial feast and that the Lord's Supper in a very real sense is a special means of grace." [75] He adds, however, that there would be "a variety of explanations of how this comes about."

The Baptist statements we have examined seem to imply that a development continues to take place from a more closed and exclusive position to one more open, and also perhaps to a more positive view of the Lord's Supper than the one traditionally found in Baptist circles.

Before we end this section, it may be of interest to add a few words about Karl Barth, who, at least as far as his view of the church is concerned, seems to belong in this context. Johnson has appealed to Barth's rejection of infant baptism. If it should so desire, Congregationalism could also appeal to Barth, especially since he holds that the Congregational order surpasses all others. In the study manual, *The Universal Church in God's Design,* published prior to the Conference in Amsterdam (1948), Barth wrote an article with the title: "The Church—the Living

[74] R. Claibourne Johnson, in Pehr Edwall *et al.* (eds.), *Ways of Worship; The Report of a Theological Commission of Faith and Order* (New York: Harper, 1951), pp. 139ff.

[75] Devadult, *op. cit.,* p. 179.

Congregation of the Living Lord Jesus Christ." [76] He says: "The objection to the *papal* church order, and, in lesser degree, also to the *episcopal, consistorial* and *presbyterian-synodal* church order, is that these systems obstruct the free access of God's Word to the actual congregation, and that they come between the congregation and the Word." To be sure, neither is the Congregational church order above criticism. "But the principle of congregationalism—the free congregation of the free Word of God—is sound enough. At any rate, certain elements of Congregationalism are absolutely indispensable for other proposals for church order if these are not to lead to disorder, but to create real order, . . . It is obvious that the last remnants of sovereign authority in the idea of a *corpus christianum* are disappearing; this suggests that we should now look in this other (Congregationalist) direction." [77]

In this chapter we have listened to a number of pronouncements about the Reformation. This review is to serve as the background for the following presentation. But the intention is not to examine and refute all the various and sometimes contradictory objections that have been voiced. The purpose of this book is not apologetic. The intention is rather to analyze the central confession of the Reformation in order to find what stands in an organic relation to it, and what does not.

[76] Karl Barth, "The Church—the Living Congregation of the Living Lord Jesus Christ," in *Man's Disorder and God's Design,* pp. 67ff.
[77] *Ibid.,* pp. 75-78.

CHAPTER 2

THE REFORMATION CONFESSION

6. *THE CONFESSION CONCERNS THE REDEMPTIVE WORK OF CHRIST IN HIS CHURCH*

The chief aim of this chapter is to provide an analysis of the Reformation confession. In the next chapter we will relate this confession to that of the Bible and that of the ancient church. Instead of isolating the Reformation, as has often been done, the intention is to place it in an "ecumenical" context. The presentation will be concentrated on the most serious concern of the Reformers. It will show that this concern involved an essential and indispensable element in the Christian message, an element which is and always will be relevant. Consequently the Reformation continues to pose questions for Christendom as a whole—and for the "Lutheran" churches as well.

When the presentation is thus directed toward the decisive element in the Reformation, and when at the same time we impose an ecumenical perspective, in the true meaning of the word, it is obvious that the result cannot be an apology that indiscriminately regards all the actions, pronouncements, and confessional formulations of the Reformation as sacrosanct. Such an isolationist attitude would abviously be contrary to the clearly expressed intention of the Reformation itself. The Reformation never claimed that its pronouncements and actions were definitive and infallible. On the contrary, it asserted as vigorously as possible that the whole question is one of an interpretation subject to the higher authority of Scripture itself. Implicit in this very claim, therefore, is the demand for continual testing on the basis of this superior norm.

No matter how much we emphasize the necessity of the Reformation, the biblical quality and Christian validity of its confession, and the tremendous values it achieved, it is doubtful that anyone would care to deny that the gain was secured at a very great price. The price, which had to be paid in full, was the deep schism of Christendom. Today we understand more clearly than in previous times how tragic the separation really was. Ecumenical efforts bear a clear witness to this fact. We may affirm at once that neither one of the partners to the conflict was without blame. But a historical attempt to assess fairly the guilt on both sides would not lead to any acceptable result. Such an attempt is of no value and ultimately meaningless. On the other hand, mutual self-examination in the present situation is both useful and necessary.

What happened was a *reformation*. The intention was not to replace the old church with a new one, but to reform the church insofar as was necessary. The purpose was to permit the gospel, which is the church's "greatest treasure," to appear in full clarity. This positive purpose was, and obviously had to be, joined with a removal of anything that tended to obscure the purity of the gospel, i.e., with "negations." In the following pages we will discuss these positive and negative aspects of the Reformation.

By way of introducton it may be proper to insert here a marginal note. It should not occasion any surprise that the men of the Reformation were not always able to carry out their program in accordance with their desire. The Reformation was like a hurricane which swept over Christendom with violent force. We may cite as an example the stand on confession. We know that Luther was uncertain in his mind as to whether confession should be regarded as a sacrament or not. But he had no doubts about its immense importance.[1] His *Small Catechism* is sufficient evidence of this fact. The intention was to provide a strong and secure place for the reformed confessional in the church. But it was by no means accorded a position commensurate with the intentions of the Reformer. Modern attempts to develop pastoral care in conjunction with confession and absolution are in agreement with the intentions of the Reformation. But they are at the

[1] Cf. Hampus Lyttken, "Biktens teologiska motivering," in *Studier,* pp. 97-114.

same time a witness to the fact that these intentions were only partially realized.

The situation is to some extent the same in regard to confirmation. The Reformers were agreed that confirmation ought not to be retained in its Medieval form. But at the same time we find the idea among many of the leading men of the Reformation that confirmation should be changed and the emphasis placed on preparatory instruction of the young.[2] These plans, however, did not lead to any immediate result. In the case of Sweden, for instance, two hundred years passed before confirmation of this kind became established in the church.

In this connection we may also note the attitude toward monasticism. Here the attitude of the Reformation was completely negative. There was no attempt to change, preserve, or "reform." In defense of this negative attitude it was pointed out that the monasteries claimed to represent a superior piety, and that in general they stood in the service of self-salvation and of "work-righteousness." This criticism may be explained on the basis that the monasticism of the time had its full share of the "decadence" of the late Middle Ages, and also on the basis of Luther's personal experience, i.e., on the basis of contemporary conditions. At the present time, as is well known, attempts are being made within both Lutheran and Reformed communions to establish monastic institutions of various kinds as centers of spiritual life and Christian activity. The criticism voiced by the Reformation is no longer relevant in this situation. No one would suggest that those connected with these attempts lay claim to a higher degree of spirituality and "holiness," or that such institutions would serve to promote the idea of self-salvation.

My presentation will obviously have to take note of the critical examination of the Reformation to which reference has already been made, and especially to the criticism issuing from Roman theology. But I have no intention whatever of writing an apology as an answer to all the various and sometimes contradictory criticisms. Many of these critical utterances can be explained on the basis of what happened later in the history of the reformed

[2] Carl-Gustaf Andrén, *Konfirmationen i Sverige under medeltid och reformationstid*, pp. 215, 218, 220, 233.

churches; as, for instance, the remarks about spiritualism and one-sided individualism. These strictures may be justified on the basis of later developments. But they would hardly have been made if these later features had not come into existence. In these cases the Reformation has been judged on the basis of later developments, and some of these features have been read into the Reformation. It is self-evident that a critical examination of the Reformation must be just that: an examination of the Reformation as it actually was. To what extent later "development" is faithful to the Reformation or departs from it is a different question.

When I think of the criticism emanating particularly from Roman quarters, I see basically only one chief objection to be raised: viz., that the Reformation considers it fundamental and essential that the living Lord is actively present in the means of grace, the Word and the sacraments. But the fundamental point of view expressed in this statement has, as we shall see, various consequences, as for example with respect to the conception of the church, Christology, the attitude of the Reformation toward Medieval passion piety, etc.

The classic expression of the Reformation confession is "justification through faith alone," *iustificatio sola fide*. This statement has been subject to many different interpretations and misinterpretations during the past centuries. In and of itself this is not surprising. It shares this distinction with many other, perhaps most other theological formulations. In view of this we must bear two things in mind. It is indisputable that the formula expresses something that the Reformation regards as fundamental and indispensable. But the formula is not what really matters. The *thing* involved is not tied to the formula, but meets us in various forms everywhere in the Reformation. It is such a living and powerful message that there can be no hesitancy about what is the heart of the matter. Furthermore, it is not a question about a single *point of doctrine*. As we have already indicated in the closing words of the previous section, the Reformation confession must be seen in the context in which it occurs. If it is separated from this context, it loses its significance and becomes misinterpreted in various ways.

In post-Reformation history we meet a number of divergent conceptions of what was the guiding principle of the Reformation. The theology of Orthodoxy conceived of Luther as the restorer of *sacra doctrina* on the basis of the authority of Scripture. The Pietistic movements emphasized the opposition of the Reformation to ecclesiastical institutionalism and interpreted it in an individualistic direction. Rationalism and Liberalism saw in the Reformation the beginning of a dissolution of the dogma of the church. Troeltsch, who had a clearer conception of the connection between the Reformation and the ancient church, and who emphasized the difference between the Reformation and "neo-Protestantism," formulated a statement which in reference to the Reformation was rather strange: "the form was the old, only[!] the content was new."

It is unquestionable that these interpretations of the significance of the Reformation were to a large extent dependent on changing conditions. To a certain extent every interpretation is dependent on contemporary presuppositions. Nevertheless it is correct to say that the intensive Reformation research in recent decades has created new opportunities for a more objective view of its meaning and its place in the history of Christianity. The relationship between the Reformation and what followed later has been more sharply defined. Sometimes the differences and the antitheses are obvious. Rationalism and its moralism stand in open conflict with the Reformation doctrine of "by grace alone." At other times, as for instance in the case of Pietism, the problem becomes much more complicated. Here it is necessary to make a fine distinction between the influence of the Reformation and influences from other sources.

There is another factor which has contributed to the creation of new opportunities for a more objective definition of the work of the Reformation: viz., modern biblical research. This has unquestionably helped to rediscover aspects of the Reformation which in time had become more or less obscured. At the same time it must be added that this biblical research has raised in a new way the question of the relation of the Reformation to the Bible.

As we have already indicated, the Reformation confession can be understood only in the context in which it stands and from which it cannot be separated. The statement about justification by faith alone is not an isolated dogma. If it is conceived of as a special point of doctrine among many others, it can be discussed back and forth forever without arriving at any understanding whatever about what the Reformation considered the ultimate concern. If it is isolated from its context, it *must* become misinterpreted; indeed, in that case it loses its meaning. What this context is we may indicate by the following thesis: The formula "justification by faith alone" is *a statement about that continuing redemptive activity which the living Christ, present and active in the Word and the sacraments, carries on in and through his church.*

The meaning of this thesis will be explicated more closely in this chapter. The following statements may serve as a preliminary orientation. Justification is an act of Christ. He, or God through him, *makes* righteous. Justification by faith alone is the same as by grace alone, by God's *agape* alone, through Christ alone. The Christ who justifies is the risen and living Lord. He acts through the means of grace, the Word and the sacraments. The means of grace are effective because Christ is actively present in them. At the same time this means that Christ carries on the work of justification in his church and through his church, and that this church is established through the means of grace through which Christ works.

The Reformation set justification by faith over against justification by works—"work-righteousness," to use its own term. We need not investigate here to what extent the Reformation's opposition to Rome was justified; whether it struck only at the corrupt practices of the later Middle Ages, or whether and to what extent it was justified also in regard to Thomist theology. We are concerned only to see *what* they were fighting against and *what* they wanted to establish. We need not be in a quandary about this. They wanted to fight against every form of self-redemption. They wanted to maintain that salvation comes to man by grace alone. "By faith alone" stands guard around the concept "by grace alone." These two formulas are inseparably connected and in reality identical. It is therefore already clear that under no circumstances can faith be understood as a human achievement which would constitute the basis of salvation. If faith were understood in this way, it would mean only that the achievement consisting in faith would be substituted for an achievement consisting in works. "By faith alone" is intended to ward off all ideas of human "merits" in connection with salvation. Its purpose is to remove everything suggestive of *meritum*. When *sola fide* is understood as a guardian of *sola gratia,* it means that faith is not concerned with human worthiness, but, in the famous and expressive words of Luther, "Faith snatches us away from ourselves and places us outside of ourselves" (*rapit nos a nobis et ponit nos extra nos*).

What is the object of faith? The answer is Christ. Here we encounter "grace." Justification by faith alone means the same as *through Christ alone.* This tells us first of all something essential about grace. It is nothing else than the love of God, God's *agape,* as this meets us in Christ and works through him. In this connection we are reminded of Melanchthon's well-known words: "Grace is not a medicine: it is God's kindness, benevolence, favor." "By faith alone" and "by grace alone" means the same as by God's *agape* alone, active in Christ.

If justification takes place through Christ alone, it means further that it is Christ who *makes* righteous. Christ is active. It is not a question simply of what Christ once did in the past, but also, and especially, of what he does now. The meaning of his activity in the present may be described in various ways. It would be misleading if we were to isolate some special expression and make that determinative for the whole. Only a total view of the varied expressions can give us a clear picture of what is involved. Salvation, justification, may be described as a bestowal of forgiveness of sins. It may also be explained by saying that man, who has no righteousness of his own, becomes a partaker of the righteousness of Christ; or that the righteousness of Christ is "imputed" to him and he is "declared" righteous. In this connection it can also be said that salvation involves "an exchange": Christ takes man's sin upon himself and gives man his own righteousness. This "exchange" means that there is communion between Christ and man. All these various expressions, and others

61

that may be used, point to the fact that we are dealing with something that Christ does for man and with man. What he does may be summarized by saying that he incorporates man into a new context of life, which has been created by his act of reconciliation finished once for all; or, in other words, into his church, "the communion of saints." The forgiveness of sins provides access to this living fellowship. But what happens means not only the removal of the burden of sin, but also participation in "life and salvation," and in all the riches contained in the context of the new life.

What we have said now about the work of salvation elucidates what is meant by salvation through *faith* alone. The act of salvation is entirely an act of Christ. This act creates faith. Faith is the sign of man's new relationship to Christ, which comes into being when man is incorporated into a living fellowship with him. Luther has a classic statement: "in faith itself Christ is present" *(in ipsa fide Christus adest)*. If "faith" therefore involves a relationship between Christ and man, it means that faith may also be considered from man's point of view. Faith means then man's *acceptance* of the gift given by Christ. This point of view eliminates completely the question as to how salvation can be partly the work of God and partly the work of man; or how it can be partly dependent on what God does, and partly on qualifying achievements on the part of man. The man whom Christ saves is an unqualified sinner. Faith cannot be understood as a qualifying, human achievement. On man's part faith is primarily receptive. But this does not mean at all that man is passive in relation to what takes place. He *participates actively* to the highest degree. From this point of view faith is man's Yes to the gift given to him on the basis of pure, undeserved grace. His acceptance of the gift means that he has been won and overcome by Christ and has been brought to *obedience* in faith under him (cf. further Chap. 4). If faith were not primarily conceived of from this point of view, but were regarded as a matter of holding more or less tenaciously to certain doctrines as true—to speak in modern terminology—"Christianity" would be transformed into an ideology, one among many ideologies competing with each other. To be sure, Christian faith includes both the acceptance of something as true and a confession. But acceptance and confession depend primarily on the fact that faith is "God's work," God's redemptive act through Christ. If this context is ignored, the truth will be lost, and faith will be devoid of meaning.

7. *THE ACTIVE PRESENCE OF CHRIST*

The formula "justification by faith alone" is a statement about that continuing redemptive activity which *the living Christ, present and active* in the Word and the sacraments, carries on in and through his church.

Since we have defined in a preliminary way what justification by faith alone means, we must look more closely at the context in which this Reformation confession occurs. The question which immediately demands our attention is concerned with the relationship between Christ's finished work of reconciliation and his continuing work in the church. Here we propose the following thesis: Salvation takes place thanks to the fact that Christ as *Kyrios* continues in his church the work of reconciliation he fulfilled on the cross. The characteristic feature of the Reformation is not only its strong emphasis on the fact that the atonement has taken place once for all but also, and especially, that it combines what once happened with that which continually takes place in the church of Christ, where Christ realizes the victory which had been won through sacrifice. He accomplishes this continuing work through the means of grace, the Word and the sacraments.

In our review of some contemporary Roman theologians' attitude toward the Reformation we found that Congar claims to have discovered a christological antithesis. He claims that as we examine the traditionally controversial questions, we encounter a christological divergence which appears to be the reason for the difference in each party's conception of the church. Congar is unquestionably right in saying that Christology, in the widest sense of the word, deserves much greater attention in this connection than it has usually received. He is also correct in saying that there is a difference, but the question is whether in defining this difference he has really discovered the essence of the matter.

Bouyer also speaks of christological differences. It is obvious, however, that the aspects these two theologians find in Reformation Christology are not the same. According to Congar the Reformation emphasized the divinity of Christ at the expense of his humanity. According to Bouyer the Reformation was greatly dependent on Medieval passion piety, which he criticizes severely. But in that case the emphasis would be on Christ's suffering humanity.

Let us remind ourselves of what Bouyer had to say about the connection between Medieval passion piety and the Reformation. His criticism of this piety and the cultic practices connected with it was that these cultic usages had developed without any thought of the risen Lord, and that Christ's human life here on earth, his suffering and death, had been isolated from his resurrection in such a way that the conception of "Christ's presence *in mysterio*" was practically eliminated. He maintains, therefore, that the Reformation point of view was in line with this passion mysticism and its emphasis on the suffering humanity of Christ. This appears, he claims, because the Reformation has made the passion memorial central in the celebration of the Lord's Supper, and even "reduced everything" to a mere memorial of his passion. The celebration of the Lord's Supper consists therefore solely in the contemplation of the sufferings of Christ even to "the total exclusion of any thought of His Resurrection." "All this," says Bouyer, "is nothing but the final development of the medieval over-emphasis on the suffering Humanity of Christ, combined with the effect of the gradual disappearance of the true idea of the liturgy as sacramental, this idea having been already buried under a merely sentimental and allegorical remembrance of the past." [3]

All this is actually a reversal of the facts. The claim that the Reformation completely excluded the resurrection and wanted to make the Lord's Supper merely a passion memorial, a sentimental and allegorical remembrance of the passion, cannot be proved in reference to Calvin, and much less in regard to Luther, for whom Christ's sacramental, active "presence *in mysterio*" was a central concern.[4] Nor does his criticism square with what Bouyer

[3] Bouyer, *Piety,* p. 42.
[4] On Luther's doctrine of the Lord's Supper see Gustaf Aulén, *Eucharist and Sacrifice,* trans. Eric H. Wahlstrom (Philadelphia: Muhlenberg, 1958), pp. 65-112.

himself says about the wideness and comprehensiveness of Luther's conception of the redemptive work of Christ, and how we find in Luther a vital intuition of Christ victorious over all things through the power of the cross and drawing us into his kingdom *through his resurrection*. Unquestionably Luther's relationship to Medieval theology and piety presents many problems. But it is quite preposterous to consider the Reformation as dependent on typical Medieval passion piety and as a development from it.

We find here instead a radical departure. Reformation piety was not interested in arousing compassion and sympathy for the martyrdom of Christ. The essential element in the Reformation proclamation is not, as in Medieval passion piety, to demand meditation on and imitation of the sufferings of Christ (*meditatio et imitatio passionis Christi*).[5] It is of course true that Luther's proclamation is a preaching of the crucified Christ. His "theology" has been described as a *theologia crucis*. That is true indeed, but his theology of the cross is a *theologia gloriae crucis Christi*. Here the resurrection has certainly not been obscured. Luther has never written a passion hymn which is not at the same time an Easter hymn. The Crucified is at the same time the risen Lord, *Kyrios*. In Luther we find this combination of cross and resurrection which was lacking in Medieval passion piety. We could quote hundreds of passages from Luther to prove that he had no intention of isolating the cross from the resurrection, but it would be impossible to find a single statement in his Reformation writings that would agree with the spirit of passion piety. In this respect his thought is in line with that of his Swedish follower, Olaus Petri, who in a Good Friday sermon criticizes the current practice of celebrating the death of Christ "with sorrowful gestures and ceremonies" in order that we "may be sorrowing and crying with Jesus, who today has suffered pain and death, and have compassion on him. We do well to be sorrowful, but not because he has suffered such pains, but because we have been the cause of his suffering all these things." [6]

It cannot indeed be denied that we may find a counterpart to Medieval passion piety even within Reformation precincts.

[5] Cf. Ulf Bjorkman, *Stilla veckan i gudstjänst och fromhetsliv* (1957).
[6] *Ibid.*, p. 335.

But these features did not appear until a couple of centuries after the Reformation. In the Pietistic and Moravian movements there appears a theology of the cross and of the wounds of Christ, which, although not identical with Medieval passion piety, nevertheless manifest a remarkable analogy to it. Here the emphasis is on the cross to the obscuring of the resurrection. Good Friday overshadows Easter. These movements come from various sources. But the principal source is unquestionably Medieval passion piety, which in various ways, especially through devotional writings and prayer books, has persisted in its influence.

All of this, however, is foreign to the Reformation. Its atmosphere is completely separated from such sentimentality. We need only listen to the strains of the great battle hymn of the Reformation, *Ein' feste Burg ist unser Gott,* to discover the fundamental difference. The same difference appears very clearly in the most classic document of the Reformation: Luther's explanation to the second article of the Creed. The very construction of this explanation is illuminating. The main clause expresses the central element in the confession: Jesus Christ "is my Lord." After this the confession states how this Lord through his finished work on the cross "has redeemed me, a lost and condemned creature, delivered me and freed me from all sins, from death, and from the power of the devil." This confessional statement stands between the *Kyrios* in the introductory words and the final words about the risen Christ. All this has taken place "in order that I might be his, live under him in his kingdom, and serve him in everlasting righteousness, innocence, and blessedness, even as he is risen from the dead and lives and reigns to all eternity." In these words there is no sentimental martyr. The explanation is a confession to that Lord who through his sacrifice, "his innocent suffering and death," has won the victory, and who actualizes his victory in that kingdom where he "lives and reigns."

The thing that especially characterizes this Reformation proclamation is its combination of what happened once for all, the finished work, with what happens ever anew among us. What happened once is not something that belongs only to the past. As Luther says, it is not a *Chronikengeschichte,* but a living and life-giving reality (*res viventes ut vivificient nos*). The atoning work

66

of Christ is something that is in the deepest sense always present, not something that has only historical results. "What happened once historically in time, when Christ came, put an end to the law and brought freedom and eternal life to light, happens now daily and spiritually in each and every individual Christian." [7] "When you look at this person [Christ], you see how sin, death, the wrath of God, hell, the devil, and everything evil has been overwhelmed and destroyed. Insofar therefore as Christ by his grace rules in the hearts of the faithful, there is no sin, no death, no condemnation." Christ is present "in faith itself," as Luther never tires of declaring. Christ "rises again" in man and performs his work. Christ is not passively present in faith. In Luther's drastic language, he "strikes and chokes" those enemies and tyrants who oppose him and his rule.

Luther's graphic picture of the living and active Lord would not be fully presented unless we also take into account what he says about the Spirit. Without any lengthy discussion we may say that *Christus-Kyrios* and the Spirit are inseparably united. The Spirit may be said to do the same work as the living Lord and to bestow the same gifts as Christ. But the work of the Spirit may also be distinguished from that of Christ. The Spirit leads men to Christ. The explanation to the third article must be read in direct connection with that of the second article.

Congar wanted to establish that the antithesis between the Reformation and the true "Catholic" conception could be traced to a christological antithesis. We have now come to the point in our presentation where it would be profitable to examine his arguments in detail in order to define the christological position of the Reformation. We may summarize his principal points as follows. According to Congar the Reformation conception of salvation as exclusively a work of God had the result that the only christological reality of any significance was the divinity of Christ. His humanity had no real significance. Naturally Congar would hold that such a Christology bore the marks of Monophysitic or at least monergistic doctrine. Furthermore this Christology was connected with a spiritual conception of salvation. There was a vacuum between Christ in heaven and man on earth.

[7] Luther, *EA*, Lat., Gal. II, p. 22.

This was because Christ did not continue his work in the visible church. Luther regarded the means of grace simply as "signs." To be sure, we may find many statements of a different nature. His talk about the Word as a means of grace has indeed true value. But, Congar insists, the statements which emphasize the effectiveness of the means of grace stand in conflict with his fundamental point of view.

It is not difficult in a sense to explain how Congar has come to interpret Luther as if only the divinity of Christ and not his humanity had a part to play in salvation. It is undoubtedly Luther's meaning that salvation is a work of God. Some classic words in his Commentary on Galatians, about how the blessing in Christ contends with the curse, express this very clearly. "Christ the power of God, righteousness, blessing, grace and life, overcomes and destroys these monsters, sin, death and the curse, without war or weapons. . . . Here you see how necessary it is to believe and confess the article of the divinity of Christ. When Arius denied this, he also had to deny the article of redemption. For to overcome the sin of the world, death, the curse, and the wrath of God himself, is not the work of any creature, but of divine power. . . . To abolish sin, to destroy death, to take away the curse in himself; and again, to give righteousness, to bring life to light, and to give blessing are the works of *divine power only and alone*." [8] According to the point of view presented in these words there can be no doubt but that divine power alone is able to carry out the work of salvation.

This does not mean, however, that Luther's Christology had a more or less Monophysitic character, or that the idea of Christ's humanity had been obscured and ceased to play any part in salvation. Luther's Christology is not at all a Docetic theophany. For him that would have involved a denial of the reality of the Incarnation. The Incarnation means that God "is hid in the despised man Jesus," as Luther often says. If we are to understand the meaning of the Incarnation, we must not start "from above" as "the philosophers and the wise in this world" do. We must rather follow Scripture as it leads us "gently" first to "Christ as to a human being and thereafter to one who is Lord over all creatures, and

⁸ Luther, *WA* 40ᴵ, 441.

then finally to one who is God." Luther returns again and again in his thinking to the human picture drawn in the Gospels. He contemplates earnestly this human life in all its lowliness, privations, trials, and suffering unto death. The central point is not in any abstract speculations about Christ's divine being, but in the concrete and historical figure who meets us in a living reality in the Gospels. Luther maintained the true humanity of Christ with as great emphasis as Chalcedon.

What distinguishes Luther's view of the redemptive work of Christ from that of the Medieval Scholastics, from Anselm down, is the fact that he does not divide the work of salvation into two parts, one being that which Christ does as God and the other that which he does as man. The work of salvation is one and indivisible. But it may be seen from different points of view. Christ is the one in and through whom God works. The God of creation and the God of redemption are one and the same God. Christ is also the one who acts in behalf of man. In solidarity with humanity he bears their burdens and endures the punishment due to sin. He does all this in obedient *fulfilment of the law*. The divine and human aspects of Christ's redemptive work are not "mixed together." But his work of redemption remains nevertheless one and indivisible. It cannot be divided in such a way that he has done something "as God" and something else "as man," for here the divine and the human are "indissolubly and inseparably united," to use the words of the formula of Chalcedon. When Congar says that Christ's "holy humanity is indeed a secondary, but nevertheless a real source of salvation," the difference between him and Luther is not that Congar says more than Luther about the significance of Christ's humanity for salvation, but rather that he says *less*. Luther never suggested that Christ's humanity should have only a *secondary* significance. The work of salvation is whole and indivisible. What he does *qua Deus* can never be separated from what he does *qua homo*.[9]

[9] Proof of the theory that a theology dependent on the Reformation tends to emphasize the divinity of Christ at the expense of his humanity has also been found in a reference to my book *Christus Victor*. One reference is in Sartory, *op. cit.*, p. 160. The purpose of this book, however, is not to contrast Christ's divinity with his humanity. The criticism of Anselm's theory is directed against his division of the redemptive work into what Christ does as God and what he does as man.

Just as everything depends on the fact that the work of salvation is "the work of the divine omnipotence," so also everything is dependent on the fact that the work of salvation is accomplished by "the despised man Jesus."

On the other hand, Congar is unquestionably right when he notes that Luther's Christology is "soteriological" rather than "ontological." Nor can we object to his statement that this aspect is "more in accordance with Semitic, prophetic, and biblical thinking than with Greek thought." In reality it was this "ontological" orientation that led Scholastic theology into the temptation to divide the redemptive work of Christ and to distinguish between what Christ did "as God" and what he did "as man." It is evident that this ontological perspective also makes other difficulties for Scholastic theology. With its terminology and concepts—*substantia,* etc.—it became difficult to maintain seriously "the true humanity" of Christ. It is noteworthy that Thomas Aquinas in his *Summa* has difficulties with such biblical expressions as "emptied himself," "humbled himself," "for our sake he became poor," and also with the realistic account of the temptation of Jesus. He finds a solution for this difficulty in distinguishing between a higher and a low stratum in the soul of Jesus. Suffering, pain, and anguish cannot reach the higher sphere; they belong only in *pars inferior* and in the body.[10]

The ontological perspective is therefore unquestionably accompanied by many hazards. But that does not mean that it should be abandoned. In spite of the evident hazards and the unsatisfactory terminology taken from Greek philosophy, the ontological perspective is to maintain something essential and indispensable, and relevant to the biblical conception of redemption. The problem may be stated this way: If the soteriological aspect is put in opposition to "the ontological," the danger is that the full meaning of salvation will be curtailed. This curtailment has not infrequently appeared in post-Reformation theology. It is found in a one-sided emphasis on the forgiveness of sin, which is conceived of as a mere remission of guilt without giving due recognition to the fact that salvation also involves "life and

[10] P. E. Persson, *Sacra doctrina, en studie till förhållandet mellan ratio och revelatio i Thomas' av Aquino teologi* (Lund, 1957), pp. 293ff.

blessedness" and fellowship with God. It is in reality this total view of salvation that the ontological perspective is designed to safeguard, when the Nicene Creed speaks of Christ in such formulas as "Light of Light, Very God of very God, of one substance with the Father," and at the same time "true man." We will return to these problems in the next chapter when we discuss the relationship of the Reformation confession to the confession of the ancient church.

We shall then take up the second of Conger's criticisms, which deals with Christ and the means of grace. These means of grace are only "signs." He claims there is a vacuum between Christ in heaven and men on the earth. The decisive point is not in the term "sign" itself. This term may be variously interpreted, and as a matter of fact it is used in referring to the sacraments in modern Roman theology. But when Congar says that the means of grace are "mere" signs, he evidently means that Christ is not conceived of as active and working in the means of grace. Congar is not alone in making this claim. But I must confess that of all the objections that have been made against the Reformation, there is none that is further removed from the truth than this one. Even Congar has to admit that in Luther we find a multitude of statements that point in another direction. Hence his final conclusion, that such positive statements are contrary to Luther's fundamental point of view, is completely without any basis in fact. Nothing is more characteristic of Luther's way of talking about the means of grace, both Word and Sacrament, than his insistent assertions that these are "means" through which Christ or the Spirit works and acts. These are not ideas which he expressed first in his contention with the "fanatics" and free spirits. They are rather something constitutive which is inseparably joined to "justification by faith alone." But of this we shall speak further.

8. THE CHURCH, THE MEANS OF GRACE, AND THE MINISTRY

The formula "justification by faith alone" is a statement about that continuing redemptive activity which the living Christ, present and active *in the Word and the sacraments,* carries on *in and through his church.*

To define the Reformation conception of the church, we may start with a "thesis" formulated by Luther himself: "The Word and the sacraments constitute and build the kingdom of Christ" (*Verbum et sacramenta constituunt et aedificant regnum Christi*). "The kingdom of Christ" is used here as a designation of the church, the church of Christ.

The reason the Word and sacraments are spoken of as creating the church is that Christ, or the Spirit, uses Word and Sacrament as means in this creative work. Everything is dependent on the fact that here the living Christ himself is active. Everything depends on the fact that the Spirit "calls, gathers, enlightens, and sanctifies the whole Christian church on earth." But just as the statement about the church-creating activity of the Word and the sacraments includes so to speak an "upward" extension, so also it includes a "downward" extension. It presupposes that there are persons who have been entrusted with the task of administering these means of grace. In this sense Luther speaks of "the ministry" of the church as "a service which proceeds *from* Christ, not to Christ, and which comes *to* us and not from us." In other words, the ministry in relation to Christ and the means of grace is altogether a ministry of service.

Word and Sacrament therefore constitute and build the church. A few words about the relationship between them may be in place at this point. When Luther speaks about the Word as a means of grace, he is introducing something new in comparison with Medieval theological tradition. In Thomas' exposition in his *Summa* of how salvation is mediated to men the sacraments alone are mentioned. It is well known that when Luther sees the Word as a means of grace, he thinks not only of the biblical Word, but also, and especially, of the preached Word. His discovery, or rediscovery, of the Word as a means of grace was inseparably connected with his firm insistence that "grace" was not some more or less indefinite, substantial power, but rather nothing else and nothing less than God's forgiving mercy. There was nothing more important than that this "most holy gospel" of God should be proclaimed clearly, freely and fully in the church, and not be shunted aside, "put under a bushel," as had been done in the church at that time.

72

Does this emphasis on the Word as a means of grace imply that the sacraments are obscured and their significance reduced? This question is relevant because a depreciation of the sacraments has unquestionably appeared in the church of the Reformation during later centuries. This has expressed itself differently in reference to Baptism and the Lord's Supper. True, the practice of baptism has been preserved, but depreciation has shown itself in the fact that the conception of baptism as an act of God has been weakened. Use of the Lord's Supper, on the other hand, has been set aside and neglected; the sermon has become the principal element in the worship service, and the Lord's Supper a more or less necessary appendage. The question is whether this "development" stems from the attitude of the Reformation itself. When Luther rediscovered the Word as a means of grace and maintained this against a conception in which the sacraments were everything, it might be argued reasonably enough that he was led to regard the sacraments as a somewhat secondary means of grace. After all, has he not actually done so? Is this not his conception when in the Smalkald Articles he speaks of the various forms of the gospel and designates the spoken Word as "the real task and ministry" of the gospel "through which the forgiveness of sin is preached in the whole world"? Or, when in the Catechisms he stresses the importance of the fact that both in Baptism and in the Lord's Supper the action is connected with the Word of God?

The answer to these questions depends entirely on what "the Word" means. This "Word" is nothing else than the "justifying" Word which Christ himself speaks. This is equally true of preaching and of the Word connected with the Sacrament. The proclamation is a word of God only because and in so far as Christ himself speaks through the human instrument. Without this the sermon consists only of human words. In the same way the Sacrament is a sacrament because in it Christ speaks and acts. The Word of Christ which meets us here is not something added to the Sacrament, but something which *inheres in* the Sacrament, something constitutive for it. But this presence of "the Word" in the Sacrament obviously does not mean that the Sacrament should be secondary to "the spoken Word." Any attempt to establish a relationship of rank between the various means of grace is foreign to Luther. Such an idea would be unthinkable since the essential element in all the means of grace is that Christ is active in them. This means that the "grace" mediated by the means of grace is one and indivisible. Wherever this grace comes to man, it comes fully and completely, not in part, and not conditioned in various ways. As Luther contended for the Word as a means of grace, so he did also for the sacraments. The purpose of the fight he fought on different fronts was to maintain their sacramental character, or, in other words, their character as real means of grace. This is true in regard to the Lord's Supper, not only in his struggle against a spiritual dissolution of the Real Presence, but also against Rome. The sacrifice of the Mass obscured the character of the Lord's Supper as a means of grace. But it could never have occurred to Luther that it would be necessary to maintain the sacraments as over against the Word as means of grace. It was indeed Christ who came in the Sacrament as well as in oral preaching based on the biblical word. Only in *one* sense could Luther have seen the Word as absolutely superior. That would be when Christ himself is identified with the Word, the incarnate Word, as set forth in the Fourth Gospel. It is possible that this biblical terminology has had a suggestive influence and has contributed in later times to a downgrading of the sacraments in relation to "the Word" as a means of grace. But in that case this is due to "the power of the Word over thought." In reality this view of the Word excludes all possibility of grading the means which Christ as the Word employs.

Just as Luther never thought of grading the means of grace so it never occurred to him to ask why different forms of the means of grace were necessary. His reaction to them is simply one of gratitude. When in the Smalkald Articles he enumerates the various forms in which the gospel meets man, and mentions not only the Word, Baptism, and the Lord's Supper, but also "the power of the keys and the mutual conversation and consolation of brethren," he introduces this enumeration with the words: "The gospel gives us in many ways assistance and help against sin *because God is abundantly rich in his grace*" (italics by Aulén). He is grateful for *all* the "help" against the powers of evil which God in his grace bestows. The question is not of what is absolutely necessary, or of what we could do without, but only of what we have received.

The Word and the sacraments "constitute and build up" the church. What church? No doubt Luther would immediately answer, the church which is "the communion of saints," *congregatio sanctorum*. A parallel to this expression is "the communion of true believers" in the eighth article of the Augsburg Confession. Does this mean that he thinks of the church in spiritual terms as an "invisible" church? This would no doubt be so if faith were conceived of as "resting in itself." But this is entirely foreign to the Reformation point of view. Faith does not rest in itself, but entirely in Christ. Since "justification by faith alone" is identical with justification through Christ alone, and since Christ in his church accomplishes his justifying work through Word and Sacrament, the church is given a secure foundation which stands in sharp contrast to all spiritualism. It is therefore by no means true that the Reformation set an "invisible" church in opposition to a "visible" one. If we examine the history of the idea of the church through the centuries, it will be clear that the terms visible and invisible church have been singularly fruitful in creating obscurity and confusion. This has been true especially when these terms have been applied to the Reformation view of the church. "Invisibility" can be spoken of only in the sense that it is not men but God alone who knows who the true believers are. But this does not mean that the church as such is invisible and unable to appear as a concrete reality existing in history. The church as the communion of saints is not something alongside of and separable from the one, holy, catholic church which came into being through Christ: it is the church of Easter and Pentecost which has existed on earth through the centuries. It is not an "inner" church in contrast to an "external" one, since the factors creating the church, the Word and the sacraments, are *concrete realities*. The church as the communion of saints is inseparably connected with their function, or, more properly stated, with that work which Christ performs through them.

What is fundamental and essential in this view of the church

75

is expressed very clearly in the exegesis of the second verse of the first chapter in Luther's large Commentary on Galatians. The commentary was written at a time when Luther's polemic against Rome was most intense. He does not mince words. In this context his words about the "holiness" of the Roman church become very important. Luther writes: "Even though the city of Rome is worse than Sodom and Gomorrah, there remains nevertheless baptism, sacrament, the gospel, the Holy Scriptures, the ministry, the name of Christ and the name of God. He who appropriates this possesses it, and he who does not is not excused, for the treasure is really there. On this account the Roman church is holy because it has God's holy name, the gospel, baptism, etc. If these things are found among a people, they are called holy. Thus also our Wittenberg is a holy city, and we are truly holy because we are baptized, have received the Lord's Supper, and have been taught and called by God. We have God's work among us, the Word and the sacraments. This is what makes us holy."

The emphasis is on this fact: we have God's work among us. Luther explains later that holiness does not depend on our achievements. "The works are indeed good," but "they do not make us holy." "I and you, the church, a city, a people are holy, not on their own account, but by the holiness of another, not through active but through passive holiness, because they have holy and divine things: viz., the call to the churchly ministry, the gospel, baptism, etc. Through these things they are holy." [11]

These words of Luther show better than long expositions what is essential in his view of the church. He can speak most violently against Rome. The Pope persecutes the gospel, he preaches the doctrines of men, the sacraments are misused. But nevertheless he declares that the Roman church is holy, because "it has God's holy name, the gospel, baptism, etc." The same is true about the church in Wittenberg. Here there is no difference. Thus Luther formulated his statement about the holy church briefly and clearly: "The church is found everywhere in the world where the gospel and the sacraments are found." Where they are found, the church does not perish, for they cannot be

---

[11] Luther, *WA* 40I, 70.

found except as they *function*. We have, he says, "God's work among us." God's work is the work of salvation. God is able to perform the work of salvation through the gospel, even though men do not "think rightly" about it. Just the same salvation is there as a work of his grace alone.

In view of these statements taken from his large Commentary on Galatians the assertion that Luther's view of the church is spiritual, subjective, or individual is obviously preposterous. The way in which the Anglican pamphlet, *Catholicity,* distinguishes between "Catholic" and "Protestant" is not relevant to this view. The sequence is not: Christ—the individual Christian—the church. If this sequence were to have any meaning, the church would have to be conceived of as in some sense an assembly, a society of individual Christians, or of "the true believers." This line of thought is completely contrary to that view in which the Word and the sacraments "constitute and build up the church." On this account Luther resists with unbending energy the attempts of *Sakramentierer, Wiedertäufer, und Rottengeister* to draw a boundary around the true believers and thus create "pure congregations." Such attempts are in vain. It is greatly presumptuous to believe one is able to decide who are the true believers. But this is not all. These attempts are in reality an attack on the existence of the church. The result of fanatics wanting to have only wheat and a pure church is that through their great holiness a sect of the devil appears instead of the church ("dass sie gar keine Kirche, sondern eine pur lautere Secte des Teufels sind").[12]

If possible an even stronger indication of how afraid Luther was of the ideal of the church represented by the "fanatics" is found in the fact that this fear actually prevented him from taking such desirable steps as might be called for in the interest of the program of the congregation and the care of souls. In the preface to *Deutsche Messe* and in some other writings from the 1520 decade Luther suggests that congregational life could be stimulated and strengthened by the organization of so-called inner circles of those who really desired to be true Christians.

[12] The quotation is from *Anmerkungen über den Evangelisten Mattheus* (1538).

It was not a question of creating a church, but of developing an organization within the congregation in the interest of establishing Christian fellowship and promoting Christian activity. There was nothing in this idea contrary to the view of the church which holds that essentially the church is built on the Word and the sacraments. Nonetheless Luther found it best to abandon this plan, and the main reason for it was his fear that such a plan would lead to *Rotterei*. It might be said that this was an unnecessary fear, and we might deplore the fact that Luther did not find a form for this plan which would have been congruous with his view of the church. In any case this episode in the history of the Reformation shows that any tendencies toward a subjective and individualistic view of the church were completely foreign to Luther.

The Medieval reform movements had opposed an individualistic conception of the church to Roman institutionalism. The Reformation did not follow their example. Its conception of the church is not individualistic. It does not conceive of the church as an assembly of believing people, to use Congar's expression. Why not? According to the Reformation the church is essentially a communion of saints, a fellowship of believers. Would not this view result in "faith" becoming the main factor in building the church? Luther says no, and he does so not to minimize faith, but rather to safeguard faith, justifying faith. The fanatics, he says, "lose the church; yes, even the gospel and Christ, and never do find any church." What arouses Luther to combat against the fanatics' conception of the church and their "pure" church is nothing else than his adherence to the doctrine of justification by faith. If the church were something secondary to faith, then "by faith alone" would not be identical with "by Christ alone." In other words, faith would be transformed into a qualifying achievement. We cannot understand the Reformation conception of the church unless we see it in its inseparable connection with the confession of "justification by faith alone." This confession speaks of the work which Christ performs in and through his church.

Now we may summarize. The church is the realm where Christ reigns, *regnum Christi*. As such it is "the communion of saints," "the fellowship of believers." Christ is its King; the church is his mystical body, *corpus mysticum*. The reign of Christ is manifested in his being the *life-giving* power in this his body. His life, his "will and work," flow from him as the Head into the members of the body (*influxus capitis in membris*). This conception of the church clearly has a sacramental character. The church is life-of-Christ's-life. It is "a kingdom of grace."

This spiritual church of Christ, this "inner Christendom," is not identical with the organized church, or "external Christendom." As far as the membership is concerned the boundaries of the inner and the external Christendoms do not coincide. No "godless and evil" belong to Christ's *corpus mysticum*. Only those belong to it who have received the gift given by Christ through Word and Sacrament. But at the same time the inner and the external Christendoms belong indissolubly together. The one cannot be thought of without the other. We could illustrate the relationship between them by the formula of Chalcedon: they are united without division, yet without confusion. No one but God can establish the boundaries around the communion of the faithful. To that extent the body of Christ is a hidden church, an *ecclesia abscondita*. It is not the object of sight or demonstration; it is an object of faith. The conviction of faith that this church lives within external Christendom rests on the fact that Word and sacraments are functioning within it; or rather, it is a conviction that here Christ is present and active through the Word and the sacraments. It is this activity that makes external Christendom something more than just a human association. On this basis it is proper, as we have already heard, to call both the church in Rome and the church in Wittenberg a "holy" church. This does not mean then that everyone within this church would be a true member of the body of Christ. Since, however, no one without usurping the place of God can presume to decide who are and who are not members, we must, according to Luther, act on the basis of brotherly love, *sub specie charitatis;* which implies that we regard every baptized person as a member of the church of Christ, as long as he has not excluded himself from the fellowship of the church.

In the light of what we have said we must finally touch on

the question of the order and the ministry of the church. The church as the body of Christ is, to be sure, to that extent an *ecclesia abscondita* around whose membership no definite boundaries can be established. But this does not mean that the church of Christ has no concrete foundation. We have already spoken of its foundation in the Word and the sacraments. It follows in this connection that the church has a divine order given by Christ, in that Christ has instituted a special service, a special "ministry" for the administration of the Word and the sacraments.

Luther's opposition to Rome is not opposition to the ministry as such. On the contrary, as we have already seen, he does not mention only the gospel, baptism, and the Lord's Supper as the factors which enable us to call the Roman church holy; he also includes here "the ministries of the church." "We call the Roman church holy and all her episcopal offices holy, although they have gone astray and the occupants of the offices are godless."

We would completely misunderstand the Reformation attitude if we thought that the important things Luther says about "the priesthood of all believers" would make the special ministry superfluous. If we were to isolate certain statements, such an interpretation would seem possible. In reality there is no question of an antithesis between the two "offices" in which one would exclude the other. His insistence on the universal priesthood has an entirely different purpose. Its thrust is directed against the narrow institutionalism which had developed within the Medieval Roman church. The criticism is directed against the tendency to divide the membership of the church into an active part, represented by the hierarchy, and a passive part, represented by the lay people; or, in other words, against the tendency to regard the hierarchical institution as primary in relation to the whole church. The priesthood of all believers means that through baptism and faith all Christians participate in the kingdom of Christ and in everything that belongs to Christ: his righteousness and holiness. Participation involves a demand and a responsibility. The demand is, as he says in connection with Romans 12:1, to present their bodies as a living, holy, and acceptable offering to God. The responsibility is to bear witness to the gospel and to perform that mutual service, the *diakonia,* which is indissolubly connected with life in the church of Christ. But the responsibility also involves maintaining the special ministry connected with the Word and the sacraments. This permanent responsibility had to be exercised *extra ordinem* by performing an ordination, when the continuity of the office was threatened by the refusal of the Roman bishops to ordain pastors for evangelical congregations. When in this connection they appealed to the fact that "necessity knows no law," it is clear that they regarded the special ministry as being of the greatest necessity.[13]

Luther insists as firmly as Rome that the office of the ministry is a divine commission given by Christ. Its function lies entirely within the spiritual realm. It has the character of a pastoral ministry in the service of the church. Its task is the preaching of the gospel, the administration of Baptism and the Lord's Supper, and the care of souls with the "power of the keys." The authority the office has in these matters it has by divine right, *iure divino*. The holder of the office has this authority as an ambassador of Christ the King, but he is not a vicar of Christ. Christ has not appointed any vicar; he reigns alone in his church.

It is required of him who is to serve in the church of Christ that he should be a member in the spiritual body of Christ. The unbeliever is unworthy of being a shepherd. He is a usurper, a wolf in sheep's clothing. This does not mean that Word and Sacrament lose their power when an unworthy person serves. Luther, like the Augsburg Confession, teaches that "the sacraments and the Word are effective by virtue of the institution and command of Christ even though they are administered by ungodly men." Thus Luther writes in *The Babylonian Captivity:* "Through the faithful God performs his work; through the unbeliever he also performs his work, but as a work foreign to the unbeliever."

The ministry of the church is one and indivisible insofar as it concerns the Word, the sacraments, and pastoral care under the power of the keys. In this respect all have the same authority; there is no difference between the various persons holding the

[13] This problem has been discussed recently by a number of Swedish theologians, among them, R. Askmark, Hj. Lindroth, R. Josefson, G. Wingren, H. Fagerberg, and G. Hillerdal; the last two are in *Studier tillägnade Hjalmar Lindroth.*

office. It is another matter, however, that according to human order (*iure humano*) there are different offices. This statement applies to the office of bishop with its special responsibilities (cf. Augsburg Confession, Article XXVIII). We must emphasize that the Reformation does not reject the idea that there is also "a human order" in the church. It is indeed necessary that such human ordinances be established. It is not necessary to follow slavishly the ordinances given in the Bible for various ministries in the church. What is essential is that such human ordinances rest on Christ's own order, and that in everything they conform to the law of Christ, which is the law of love. Thus the communal life is regulated in the spirit of brotherly love, which unites Christian freedom with Christian service in an indissoluble unity.

The Reformation criticism against Rome does not attack the idea that there is a divine order in the church. Neither does it object to human ordinances. The conflict with Rome concerned primarily canon law and its application. The objection of the Reformation was that Rome not only had transformed human law into divine law, but also that it had developed and applied this human law in conflict with divine law. This had taken place in that Rome, instead of "rejecting doctrines contrary to the gospel," had brought in human doctrines contrary to the gospel. "The hierarchy" had thus taken upon itself an authority which belongs exclusively to Christ as the Head of the church.

9. *THE ESCHATOLOGICAL PERSPECTIVE*

Everything the Reformation says about justification is incorporated into an eschatological perspective. This does not mean merely that everything is oriented toward the fulfilment to come, but also that the eschatological aspect belongs to what happens now in the present, because justification means participation in the life belonging to *the new age* which has come in and through the finished, redemptive work of Christ.

Justification is mediated through the forgiveness of sin. That it takes place in this form means that salvation is at the same time judgment and forgiveness, radical judgment and radical forgiveness through God's unmerited *agape*. This twofold aspect of salvation stems from the fact that the gospel of God is inseparably connected with God's *law*. The gospel's act of forgiveness pre-supposes and appears in the light of the judgment on sin which God's law pronounces. This is the universal law of creation which never ceases to function, and which can function "anonymously" in the human community, even when man is not clearly conscious of what actually transpires in that which happens.[14] The radicalism of this judgment is revealed in Christ through his perfect fulfilment of the law. This twofold aspect of salvation is given classic expression in Luther's description of the meaning of baptism as dying with Christ and rising with him again. But the same twofold aspect is seen also in the Word and in the Lord's Supper as means of grace.

If forgiveness is the form in which salvation comes to man, it would be entirely wrong to assume that this is merely a so-called forensic declaration of righteousness.[15] Forgiveness is not simply negative. It does not stand by itself, but is connected with "life and salvation" according to the well-known words of the Catechism: "where there is forgiveness of sins, there is also life and salvation." This happens because Christ comes to us, deals with us, and enters into fellowship with us. He comes, says Luther, "not poor and destitute—he brings with him every-thing that he is, has, and can do." He makes us participate in this. He gives himself to us, "that we may possess him so com-pletely that all he has and owns becomes ours."[16] These words are characteristic of the vivid and personal way in which Luther expresses what in a more abstract theological formula reads: participation in an alien righteousness (*aliena iustitia*).

[14] Gustaf Wingren, *Skapelsen och lagen* (Lund, 1958), pp. 68ff.

[15] Cf. Lauri Haikola, "Rättfärdiggörelsen i Apologien och Konkordie-formeln," in *Studier,* pp. 51-62. Haikola points out that a shift took place because the Formula of Concord understood the words *regenerari* and *vivificari* in an exclusively forensic sense. "It therefore became more difficult to express the true idea found in the Apology that justification by faith alone means not only a change in man's objective status but also a subjective, personal experience of what this change in the objective sit-uation means for the individual. In this respect Formula of Concord III represents an impoverishment in contrast with Apology IV." *Ibid.,* pp. 61-62.

[16] The quotation is taken from H. Ivarson, *Predikans uppgift* (Lund, 1956), pp. 22 and 33 (from the Christmas Postil [1522] and the Advent Postil [1529]).

From this point of view justification by faith alone, through Christ alone, involves possessing. "He who believes has." He "has" Christ with all that he is, owns, and can do. Because this is so, Reformation preaching and hymns are filled with the joy and confidence of faith. The life of faith is a life "in Christ," "in the Spirit." God's gift, salvation and adoption as sons, is a gift given to man now in the present. We can speak here with a modern expression of "realized eschatology."

But this certainly does not mean that perfection has been reached here under the conditions of earthly life. It means rather that we look away from the present imperfection to the perfection of the world to come. The gift given in the present and "the possession" of it by faith are an earnest of what is to come in the world of fulfilment. The eschatological perspective of the Reformation is twofold: it is to an equal degree oriented both to the present and to the future.

There is a Reformation formula which is well suited to explicate the relationship between these two aspects of the Christian life. This is the famous and much debated formula which says that the justified man is at the same time a sinner and righteous, *simul iustus et peccator.* The formula is a statement concerning the Christian relationship with God. Its primary purpose is to stand guard around the confession of justification through Christ alone and through God's *agape* alone. It seeks to ward off ideas which would obscure and nullify this fundamental confession of the Reformation. What the formula wants to say about the Christian relationship with God is that this relationship always depends on and has its foundation in the forgiveness of sins. This is something, therefore, that does not have reference only to the beginning of the Christian life, to *initium,* but is true of Christian life as a whole under the conditions of human life here on earth. Man never comes to a point where he has so qualified himself that by his own attitude and his own work he could present his "own" righteousness before God. Before God, *coram deo,* he is always a sinner who has nothing else to trust in than God's mercy which meets him in the forgiveness of sins. He is not partly a sinner and partly righteous. He is altogether a sinner, who lives by and finds his righteousness in the grace of God which is new every morning.

This insistence on the Christian as a sinner does not mean that Luther has excluded "works" from the Christian life, as Congar in his study of Luther has also clearly seen. On the contrary Luther combines works closely with the life of faith. If Christ is "present in faith itself," and if the Christian life is a life "in Christ" and "in the Spirit," then Christ and the Spirit are active in the life of faith. Luther can speak therefore most emphatically about faith as "a living, powerful, and active thing." Man is justified by faith alone, but faith is really never "alone." From this point of view justification means that man is incorporated into the realm of divine love and becomes an instrument for the divine love which desires to use him in service to the neighbor. The liberation is a liberation to serve and in obedience to God's commands to deal with the neighbor in the way love demands in the various circumstances of life. As Luther often expresses it, it is a call "to be a Christ to the neighbor." The antithesis between Luther and traditional Roman theology is not that Roman theology talks about works connected with faith whereas Luther does not. Luther speaks as much as anybody about the connection between faith and works. But nevertheless by his formula, *simul iustus et peccator,* he reveals his opposition to the traditional statement of faith formed through love *(fides caritate formata)* because he rejects radically every suggestion of "merit" connected with these works. It is not a question about any merits of man produced through divine grace, and there is no "infused love" which would enable man to produce meritorious works. There is no question at all of any merits before God.

The formula, "at the same time righteous and a sinner," stands as an effective guardian for the idea, "by grace alone." But it has also another function. It stands guard as well against all tendencies to anticipate and claim in advance what belongs to the world of fulfilment. The justifying faith which means "possession," which "has Christ," and which participates in his victory over sin and death, is inseparably connected with hope. Faith cannot exist without hope, or vice versa. When Luther expounds Galatians 5:5 in his Commentary, he distinguishes

85

between faith and hope, but at the same time he says that "there is such a close relationship between them that the one cannot be separated from the other." We are justified, he says, *through Christ alone.* "When I have laid hold on him by faith, I wrestle against the fiery darts of the devil, and I take a good heart through hope against the feeling of sin, assuring myself that I have a perfect righteousness prepared for me in heaven. So both of these sayings are true: I am righteous already by that righteousness which has been begun in me; and also I am encouraged in the same hope against sin and wait for the full consummation of perfect righteousness in heaven." Hope is "a general or captain in the field who fights against tribulation, the cross, impatience, weakness, desperation and blasphemy, and lives in joy and spiritual strength." Hope is "the spiritual courage, as faith is the spiritual wisdom." [17]

When we look at "the righteousness that is our hope," we do not deny the fact that we possess righteousness now in the present. But what characterizes this present righteousness from our human point of view is partly that it is imperfect, and partly that it is hidden from our eyes. It is, says Luther, a righteousness "which you have in faith, although it is only begun and imperfect until it shall finally be revealed as perfect and eternal."

If someone says that he does not "feel" this, Luther answers: "You are not to feel but to believe that you have this righteousness. And if you do not believe that you are righteous, you insult Christ who has cleansed you in the washing of water with the Word, and who through his death on the cross has condemned and killed sin and death, in order that through him you should find righteousness and life."

Luther understands the Christian life as a struggle. The hope which sustains us in this struggle has its foundation in faith, because this is directed toward Christ. "In the midst of terror and tribulation he awakens the hope which perseveres and overcomes evil." Faith may appear only as a smoking flax, but those who in such a struggle hope and believe "will finally see that this spark of faith, which to human understanding seems so

[17] Luther, *Commentary on Galatians,* trans. Erasmus Middleton (Grand Rapids, Mich.: Zondervan, 1930), pp. 434ff.

miserably impotent because it can hardly be seen, becomes nevertheless a tremendous fire, which fills the whole heaven and devours all terror and all sins." [18]

We must understand Luther's view of sanctification against the background of what has been said about the Christian life as a struggle. His ideas on *sanctificatio* have often been the object of criticism, as we have already noted. Congar seeks to prove that justification does not result in any change in man, which means that it is not accompanied by any sanctification. *Catholicity* speaks of "the radical error," consisting in the separation of justification from sanctification. Such objections have been made not only by "Catholics." Wesley also, the founder of Methodism, who gives unqualified approval to Luther's doctrine of justification by faith alone, holds that Luther was "ignorant and confused" about the doctrine of sanctification. [19] Such objections unquestionably are due to the fact that Luther's doctrine of justification has been understood exclusively as forensic. In other words, the critics have not realized the whole positive content of forgiveness as understood by Luther. They have not observed that for Luther it is essential to see the Christian life as a struggle.

In reality it is not at all true that Luther separated and isolated sanctification from justification. On the contrary, the two are inseparably united to such an extent that in reality it is a question of one and the same thing, seen to some extent from different points of view. In both cases we are really concerned with the work of redemption which Christ carries on in his church through the Word and the sacraments. The presence of Christ in faith, of which Luther speaks, is not a passive presence. Just as "righteousness," as we have noted previously, may be seen from either of two points of view, so also may "holiness." The righteousness and holiness given to man is from one point of view participation in Christ's own righteousness and holiness, and as such they are without want or flaw. Participation in these means participation and full membership in "the communion of saints."

[18] *Ibid.*, p. 439.
[19] Cf. Philip Watson, "Luther och helgelsen," in *Svensk teologisk kvartalskrift*, 1957, p. 24.

But at the same time, when righteousness and holiness are seen from man's point of view, they are only something begun and imperfect and becoming.

But the fact that we are dealing with something that remains imperfect under the conditions of human life is not saying that in general there is no change in man. To make such a claim would mean to Luther that Christ and the Spirit were eliminated from the Christian life in faith. That the union by faith with Christ and the Spirit could leave man indifferent and remaining in the old state certainly could never have occurred to Luther. We need only remind ourselves of his words about the meaning of baptism in the *Small Catechism*. The act of God which took place in baptism has meaning for the whole of life. Its meaning is that the old man is to be drowned and destroyed through daily sorrow and repentance, and that a new man is to arise daily. But, it could be said, such a view of the matter means that man never gets any place, and that in reality this is nothing but a permanent beginning. This is evidently what is meant by the charge that justification is separated from sanctification, and that the latter loses its significance. In reality Luther thinks of sanctification from two points of view. Both of these viewpoints are combined in a statement like this: "To go forward is always to begin anew." It is a question of a continual beginning and also of "going forward." These two do not stand in conflict. Luther speaks in clear and strong words about the Christian life as advance and growth in grace, faith, and obedience. The Holy Spirit accomplishes sanctification by "obliterating, destroying, and killing sin." Here on earth there is "a Christian and holy people in whom Christ lives, works, and reigns *per redemptionem,* through grace and forgiveness of sin—and the Holy Spirit *per vivificationem et sanctificationem,* through daily washing away of sin and daily renewal—so that we do not remain in sin, but can and ought to live a new life in all kinds of good works, as God's Ten Commandments demand." [20] By these means man grows in sanctification and becomes more and more a new being in Christ. This growth in sanctification, in faith and obedience, continues throughout life. It takes place through the use of

[20] Luther, *WA* 50, 625.

God's Word and the Lord's Supper, which are the means the Spirit employs in sanctification.

In what sense then does he speak of a continual beginning? The answer is that the Christian life never reaches a point where it can build on anything else than God's forgiving grace that is new every morning. The struggle against the power of sin is so far from diminishing and ceasing that, on the contrary, growth involves a more sensitive consciousness of sin. The more righteous a person is, the more keenly he experiences this struggle (*imo quo quisque magis pius est, hoc plus sentit illam pugnam*). What this thoroughly realistic view of the Christian life rejects is not a growth toward the goal, but perfectionism which unrealistically idealizes the Christian life and ignores the actual conditions of life here on earth. Luther would regard this as an anticipation of that which belongs to the world of fulfilment. No growth in grace, faith, and obedience can alter the fact that under the conditions of life on earth man remains *simul iustus et peccator*. The life the believer has is a life in becoming, *"im Werden."* Luther's picturesque and classical words are as follows: "nit ein frumkeit, szondern ein frumb werden, nit ein gesuntheit, szondern ein gesunt werden, nit ein wesen, sunderen ein werden, nit ein ruge, szonderenn ein ubunge, wyr seyns noch nit, wyr werdens aber. Es ist noch nit gethan und geschehenn, es ist aber ym gang und schwank. Es ist nit das end, es ist aber der weg, es gluwet und glintzt noch nit alles, es fegt sich aber allesz." [21]

Finally, the statement, "at the same time righteous and a sinner," applies also to the church as a whole. The church is at the same time holy and sinful, *simul sancta et peccatrix*. In the preceding section we heard Luther speak in this way of the church both in Rome and in Wittenberg. Since no member of the church can be justified without at the same time being a sinner, the sinfulness of the church is obvious. Its holiness depends on the work of God which Christ and the Spirit perform through the means of Word and Sacrament. We remind ourselves from what was said before that Luther in this connection pointed also to "the ministries of the church" as an indication

[21] Luther, *WA* 7, 337.

of the existence of the holy church. Though even the ministerial office itself may be called holy, this does not mean that those who have been called to service in the church have been given a special holiness superior to that of the other members of the church. What is holy is the divine commission itself to serve the members of the church with Word and Sacrament. The call to this service involves a special responsibility, above all rightly to preach the gospel and administer the sacraments. But this call to service does not include any infallibility of the *magisterium,* either for the office as a whole or for any one of its occupants.

Congar, too, spoke of the church as being at the same time holy and sinful. According to him holiness appears in the structure of the church. He points to the fundamental content of faith *(depositum fidei),* the sacrament of faith, and the apostolic commission. In a certain sense Luther, too, spoke of a "structural holiness." In that case he would point to the gospel as we find it in God's Word, to the sacraments, and he would not—as we have seen—neglect to point to the divine commission of the office and service of the ministry. But he would not combine the apostolic ministry with any infallibility. This would involve a usurpation of that perfection which no man can possess under the conditions of human life on earth. It would be an attempt to take the place of Christ and the Spirit.

THREE CONFESSIONS OF CHRIST: THOSE OF THE BIBLE, THE ANCIENT CHURCH, AND THE REFORMATION

10. *THE BIBLICAL CONFESSION OF CHRIST: CHRISTUS-KYRIOS*

The purpose of this chapter is to elucidate the relationship of the Reformation confession to the biblical and to that of the ancient church. The biblical, apostolic confession is the primary and fundamental confession of Christianity. The two others are defensive confessions.

The apostles were sent out to proclaim the "gospel" in all the world. The gospel is a message, a kerygma about salvation through Christ and about the new age, the age of "the new covenant" which has come through him. This apostolic message we find collected in the New Testament. But the apostolic kerygma is at the same time a witness and a *confession*. It is from this point of view that we look at it here. We find in the New Testament a diversified confession, expressed in different ways in the various biblical writings, but at the same time unanimous and homogeneous. This apostolic confession of Christ stands incorporated in the great context of the history of salvation, which extends from the creation to the final consummation. Christ is the mid-point. The "old covenant" had been the time of the law and the promises. The "new covenant" is the time of fulfilment, both in the sense that Christ has fulfilled the law, and that the promises spoken in the Old Testament have been fulfilled in him. "For all the promises of God find their Yes in him" (II Cor. 1:20). God's activity all the way from the creation on has been consummated in Christ.

We find the biblical confession in a concentrated form as a confession to Christ as *Kyrios, Lord.* In addition to the name *Kyrios* there are in the New Testament a number of other titles of honor, such as Messiah, Son of Man, the Suffering Servant, High Priest, Savior, the Word (Logos), Son of God, God. Each one has something essential to say about Christ and his work—indeed about both of these, for the biblical confession is at the same time a confession both to the person and to his work. The two are inseparably united.

But among all these designations the title *Kyrios* is unique. This is already apparent in the fact that it occurs more frequently in the New Testament than any other. *Kyrios* as it were gathers up and includes all the other titles. This is the name that seemed to come naturally when people in the ancient church spoke of Christ. The ancient prayer, *Maranatha,* indicates that this title had been in use before the gospel extended out from Palestine into the Greek world. It was from the beginning the central confession of the ancient church. The name pictures the relationship in which the church stands to Christ. He is the living Lord of the church. When the apostles and the ancient church hail him as Lord, they give him a name which the Old Testament used about God. It is significant that many statements about God the Lord, for example in the Psalms, are simply transferred and applied to Christ. But in reality and according to their own statements it was not the *apostles* who had given him the name *Kyrios;* it was God who had "highly exalted him and bestowed on him the name which is above every name" (Phil. 2:9). The lordship which Christ thus assumed is universal. It embraces all things. "All authority in heaven and on earth has been given to me" (Matt. 28:18). But Christ exercises this power and authority primarily in and through his church, which is inseparably joined with him. A number of New Testament expressions testify to this fact; such as the church as the Body of Christ, the vine and the branches, the temple of living stones in which Christ is the cornerstone, the church as the Bride of Christ, and so forth.

Christus-Kyrios does not belong to the past. He lives and works in his church. It can also be said that his activity is carried on through the Spirit. The indissoluble union between Christ and the Spirit can be described in various ways. The Spirit is the Spirit of Christ. But it can also be said that the Lord is the Spirit (II Cor. 3:17). The church is one and indivisible because it has only one Lord. The church is the communion of saints, not because its members are perfect, but because they share in the holiness and righteousness of *Christus-Kyrios*. Participation in salvation is obtained by being incorporated into the church which is the body of Christ. This takes place in baptism. To live in the church is to live "in Christ," "in the Spirit," in a living fellowship *(koinonia)* with the living Lord.

The salvation which is thus proclaimed and experienced is completely tied in with Christ and his work. "There is salvation in no one else" (Acts 4:12). Salvation is also a wholly undeserved gift. The formula is, "by grace you have been saved" (Eph. 2:5). The condition on which this grace of God can be received is that the message of Christ be proclaimed (Rom. 10:14 ff.). Christ and the salvation he brings are received in faith. Salvation through Christ stands therefore in contrast to salvation by "works of the law," and in general is opposed to the idea that salvation is something man himself can procure. This involves a radical denial of the law as a means and way of salvation. But it does not mean that God's law is dethroned. On the contrary, Christ has fulfilled the law: both in the sense that he assumed the judgment and curse of the law, and in the sense that he has fulfilled the law and thereby become "our righteousness" (I Cor. 1:30). To have a share in his righteousness means also to be placed under the law of God, which has been made alive by Christ, under the law of Christ, the law of the Spirit! [1]

The confession of Christ as *Kyrios* is relevant to what happens in the church of Christ. Here he exercises his function as *Kyrios*. The whole life of the church receives its character from

[1] Ragnar Bring, "Mose lag och Kristus," in *Svensk teologisk kvartalskrift*, 1957, p. 150; and *Commentary on Galatians* (Philadelphia: Muhlenberg, 1961).

the work of Christ, or the Spirit. The believer turns to *Christus-Kyrios* in prayer and supplication, convinced that, according to his promise, he is with his own "to the close of the age."

The confession of *Christus-Kyrios* is a confession of the risen and living Lord. It was the resurrection that primarily and definitively prompted this confession. The evangelists testify indeed that the apostles had already made a confession of Christ during his earthly ministry: the confession of Peter at Caesarea Philippi (Matt. 16:16), and his confession of Jesus as "the Holy One of God" (John 6:69). But the Gospels also show how this confession was thoroughly shaken by Jesus' suffering and death on the cross. What the two disciples on the way to Emmaus say indicates their disappointment: "But we had hoped that he was the one to redeem Israel" (Luke 24:21). The resurrection gave new life to the confession, and at the same time a new content.

The resurrection illumines the cross. It reveals that the cross was not defeat and destruction, but victory; and that the Messiah had to go the way of suffering and sacrifice in order to "enter into his glory" (Luke 24:26). The whole New Testament content is written with the resurrection as the center and starting point. The resurrection is the light which illumines and clarifies the meaning of Jesus' earthly life and of the work finished on the cross. The apostles became the witnesses of the resurrection. What Acts says about the election of a successor to Judas is very significant: " 'So one of the men who have accompanied us during all the time that the Lord Jesus went in and out among us, beginning from the baptism of John until the day he was taken up from us—one of these men must become with us *a witness to his resurrection'* " (Acts 1:21-22).

The resurrection manifests the victory of Christ. But this victory has been won by suffering and sacrifice through the work finished on the cross. Because Christ "humbled himself and became obedient unto death, even the death on a cross, therefore God has highly exalted him and bestowed on him the name which is above every name, that . . . every tongue [should] confess that Jesus Christ is Lord to the glory of God the Father" (Phil. 2:8 ff.). Thus the apostolic confession of Christ ties the cross and the resurrection indissolubly together. The question as

94

to which one should be emphasized most is wholly irrelevant. This question, mostly unexpressed, has frequently been in the background of and has exercised an influence on the interpretation of the work of Christ. But from the point of view of the apostolic confession it is meaningless. In this confession everything depends on the unity of cross and resurrection. The one is nothing without the other. We may also state the matter in this way: Everything depends on the sacrifice finished on the cross, because in it is victory and reconciliation. Everything depends on the resurrection, for it is not only the manifestation of the victory but also transition to the never-ceasing, continual work of Christ in the church. This synoptic view of the cross and the resurrection may be expressed very clearly if we set side by side two characteristic words of Paul in his first letter to the Corinthians. His preaching in Corinth, he says, had been characterized by the fact that he "decided to know nothing among you except Jesus Christ and him *crucified*" (I Cor. 2:2). At the same time he says: "If Christ has not been *raised,* then our preaching is in vain and your faith is in vain" (I Cor. 15:14). There is no contradiction between these two statements. We find the synthesis in Romans 4:25: Christ "was put to death for our trespasses and raised for our justification."

We have seen now that the apostolic confession has its starting point in the resurrection and in that which takes place in the church of Christ, but also that what takes place in the church of Christ has its presupposition in that which took place during the earthly ministry of Jesus and in that work which was finished on the cross. In reality it is not satisfactory to speak of that which has taken place as only a presupposition. The relationship between what happens and what has happened is much more intimate. What happens in the church means really that what did happen is continually realized anew in the church of Christ. The "reconciliation" which came through the finished work of Christ happened "once for all" (Heb. 9:12, 26). It is a reconciliation of universal and cosmic scope. "He is the expiation of our sins, and not for ours only but also for the sins of the whole world" (I John 2:2). It is an "eternal" redemption. But just because it is eternal, it is always relevant and valid. Through

95

the risen and living Lord it is always present, in Baptism as well as in the Lord's Supper. Baptism means participation both in the sacrifice of Christ's death and in "the power of his resurrection." The same is true of the fellowship and *koinonia* with Christ which is realized in the Lord's Supper.

But we have not yet taken into account the whole comprehensive perspective of the history of salvation which is connected with the apostolic confession. From the synoptic view of cross and resurrection, of that which has been done once for all and of that which continually takes place in the church of Christ, we look forward and backward and span the whole comprehensive action which began with the creation and ends with the consummation. We look both to that which is going to happen and to that which has happened "from the beginning." [2]

We look forward to that which is to come, the eschatological consummation. Just as forcefully as the New Testament emphasizes salvation as something which happens in the present, so it points forward to the fulfilment which is to come when this imperfect is transformed into perfection. Salvation in the present fellowship with Christ is a liberation from the bonds of sin and a passing from death to life. "Behold, now is the acceptable time; behold, now is the day of salvation" (II Cor. 6:2). The new age, the age of fulfilment, has come in Christ as "the first fruits of those who have fallen asleep." To this extent the Christian lives already in "the last times." From this point of view eschatology is a "realized eschatology." But this does not mean that the old age has disappeared. The new life is lived in a continual struggle with sin and death. The reign of *Christus-Kyrios* is realized in that he advances in the conflict with these powers. "He must reign until he has put all his enemies under his feet" (I Cor. 15:25); i.e., until sin has been definitely eradicated and death fully overcome. To have a share in salvation means from this point of view to have a share in hope: "in this hope we were saved" (Rom. 8:24). The return of Christ to judgment marks the end of this period of struggle as *Kyrios,* and at the same time

[2] Oscar Cullmann, *The Christology of the New Testament,* trans. Shirley C. Guthrie and Charles A. M. Hall (Philadelphia: Westminster, 1959), pp. 109ff., 247ff.

it is the transition to the new creation through which imperfection is succeeded by perfection in glory.

As the confession of Christ points to that which is to come, so also it looks back to that which has been from "the beginning." This means primarily that the event of Christ is incorporated into the dramatic context of salvation which includes God's election of Israel and his dealings with them. The event of Christ stands as the end and goal of this salvation drama. It is the fulfilment of the promises given through "the law and the prophets." This connection with what had happened before in God's history with Israel is indicated also by the fact that the church which is the body of Christ is called "the new Israel."

But the perspective of this history of salvation expands further. It is not tied in only with the chosen people. It is concerned also with what happened "in the beginning," and therefore becomes universal. Christ is the Word, *Logos,* who in the beginning was with God and was God. The Johannine prologue, that all things "were made through him," is not peculiar to John. The same view is found in Paul and in Hebrews. We must note two things here. First, that here too the confession of Christ is a confession about his function, about the work of Christ. Second, creation and salvation—the work of God and the work of Christ—are inseparably joined.

As we summarize what has been said about the apostolic confession of Christ, it will appear that the confession has a fourfold aspect. It is concerned with what happens in the present in the church of Christ, where the living Lord is continually active. It is concerned with the act Christ performed during his life on earth, and finished on the cross. It turns our attention ahead to the eschatological fulfilment; and finally, it simultaneously calls attention to God's history with Israel and to that which happened "in the beginning," at creation.[3] The apostolic confession of Christ may be likened to a majestic symphony in four parts, in which the various instruments play to the honor of Christ.

We have seen that the apostolic confession is anchored primarily in the Easter experience of the disciples and in their experiences in Christ's church. It is here that the confession was re-

[3] *Ibid.,* pp. 315ff.

newed and developed in its comprehensive perspective of the history of salvation. It was renewed, but it did not originate here. As the Gospels clearly indicate, it had its beginning in the disciples' association with Jesus during his earthly ministry. The beginning of the confession is therefore unquestionably connected with Jesus' own consciousness of his calling, as this was indicated by him and appeared in word and action. Oscar Cullmann in his book, *The Christology of the New Testament,* has made a careful study of this matter. He has connected it with a number of "christological titles" which occur in the New Testament, especially Messiah, *Ebed Yahweh,* and Son of Man. In regard to the Messiah there is at least *one* aspect which has a connection with Jesus' consciousness of his call: the very fact that the Messiah realizes the purpose of Israel. The Messianic idea emphasizes the continuity between the work of Jesus and the election of Israel to its historical destiny. This continuity found its peculiar development later in Jesus' consciousness of his call. Without using the term *"Ebed Yahweh"* directly as a designation for himself, Jesus interpreted his work under the aspect of "the Suffering Servant of the Lord," both in regard to the vicarious suffering of death and in regard to the covenant between God and his people reestablished by *Ebed Yahweh.* Finally Jesus used the title Son of Man for himself both eschatologically and in reference to his earthly ministry. This title speaks of both exaltation and humiliation. With this name Jesus has expressed his conviction that he has come to perform the work of "the heavenly man," both in glory at the end of the world, and in the humility of incarnation into the world of sinful humanity. Thus the apostolic confession in the last analysis rests on the indications Jesus himself gave about his own consciousness of his calling.[4]

If now for a moment we turn our attention to the christological debates in the ancient church and to its theologically formulated confessions, or to the atonement doctrine of a later time, as for instance that of Anselm, there appears at once an obvious difference between these and the apostolic confession of the New Testament. In the latter the problem of the relationship between "the divinity" and "the humanity" of Christ does not appear.

[4] *Ibid.*, pp. 78, 126ff., 152ff., 163.

Nor do we find any attempt to distinguish between what Christ does as God and what he does as man. Instead we find a thoroughly integrated point of view.

The biblical confession asserts that the man Jesus is *Kyrios*. The question as to whether the Bible asserts "the divinity" of Christ cannot be reduced to a consideration of the relatively few passages in which Jesus is expressly called "God." The central name *Kyrios* already expresses everything; other titles do not add anything essential. As *Kyrios* Christ is the divine Lord who is the object of prayer and supplication. But this *Kyrios* is no one else than the crucified Jesus of Nazareth. The apostles who had walked with him during his earthly ministry could not doubt his "true humanity." The biblical authors, John and Paul, seriously contended against "Docetic" ideas which tended to obscure the concrete humanity of Jesus. The Christian confession means that "Jesus has come in the flesh" (I John 4:2; cf. I Cor. 11:26). But the question of how "the divine" and "the human" are related in the person of Christ was not asked by the apostolic confession. It was foreign to its thinking. The person of Christ was one and indivisible.

The same holds true in regard to the redemptive work of Christ. That, too, is one and indivisible. But the biblical authors do view this one work from two points of view: as performed on behalf of man, and as performed on behalf of God. From one point of view the redemptive and reconciling work finished on the cross is an act done by Christ on behalf of humanity, a vicarious act. In solidarity with humanity Christ assumed its burden. He accepted the punishment and the divine judgment that rested on this sinful race. In obedience to the will of his heavenly Father he fulfilled God's law even to his sacrificial death on the cross. All this was done "for our sake" and "in our stead." But at the same time this act of salvation took place on behalf of God; yes, it is God himself who in and through Christ does the work of salvation, as Paul expresses it in his classic statement: "God was in Christ reconciling the world to himself" (II Cor. 5:19). The redemptive act of Christ is God's own act. In the New Testament writings, therefore, the word "Savior" is used of both God and Christ. Redemption is a work of the God of creation. This synoptic view of the two perspectives is the essential element in the New Testament view of Christ's redemptive work. The one cannot be separated from the other without distorting the total conception. What unites them is the struggle against the enemies of humanity—sin, death, and the devil—which Christ waged both on behalf of humanity and on behalf of God, a struggle that led to the cross on which the victory was won.

The answer to our final question, as to how the apostolic confession conceives of the connection between God and Christ, must be that it is at the same time a matter of identity and a matter of relationship. Both of these aspects meet us in the Johannine prologue: "The Word *was* God," and "The Word was *with* God." [5] The identity between God and Christ is an identity of action and revelation. Faith is not divided between God and Christ; it is not a question of there being different "objects of faith." "I and the Father are one" (John 10:30); "He who has seen me has seen the Father" (John 14:9); "No one has ever seen God; the only Son, who is in the bosom of the Father, he has made him known" (John 1:18). From the point of view of revelation the connection between the Father and the Son is a matter of pure identity. Christ is God's self-revelation, his self-impartation. It is thus a matter of identity, but of an identity which does not eliminate the matter of relationship. This matter of relationship appears in the very fact that from one point of view the work of Christ is a work on behalf of humanity, and to that extent an act directed toward God. The matter of relationship appears further in the fact that the Son is "begotten of the Father," "has come from God," and also in the fact that, when the end comes, "he delivers the kingdom to God" (I Cor. 15:24). Thus the biblical confession of Christ characterizes the matter of the relationship between the Father and the Son through reference to "the beginning" and "the end."

I will close this chapter with a few words of summary. The New Testament confession is a confession of Christ. It is natural that it should be so. The new, revolutionary message which the apostles went out to proclaim was the gospel of God's saving act *in Christ.* But just as forcefully as the New Testament maintains

[5] *Ibid.,* pp. 265ff.

that the old has passed away and something new has appeared, it bears witness to the unity between this event and the events of God's previous dealings with Israel and the world even from creation. The apostolic christological confession is not an isolated confession of Christ. It cannot be emphasized enough that to the apostles as to Jesus himself the Old Testament was the Bible, *the holy Scriptures.* From this point of view the apostolic confession appears as *an interpretation of the Bible,* a new interpretation of the Old Testament. According to this interpretation the Old Testament bears witness to Christ as Messiah and *Kyrios.* In other words, the confession of Christ is the key that, so to speak, opens the sealed Scripture and permits its true meaning to appear. Or, to use Paul's figure, it removes "the veil" and discloses "the mystery which was kept secret for long ages but is now disclosed" (Rom. 16:25-26). The New Testament confession is a new message, but it is incorporated in the context of the history of salvation to which—rightly understood—the Old Testament bears witness. It can be understood only in this context, just as the Old Testament, on the other hand, can be correctly understood only by using the confession of Christ as the key.[6]

11. *THE ANCIENT CHURCH'S CONFESSION OF CHRIST: THE INCARNATION*

The confession of the ancient church as we find it in the Apostles' Creed and in a fuller form in the Nicene Creed, is not only a confession of Christ. These two classic creeds of the church have a trinitarian form. This trinitarian aspect is not something new in reference to the New Testament. This is evident, not only on the basis of sporadic trinitarian formulas in the text, but also on the basis of what is said about the Father and the Spirit. We previously emphasized that the New Testament confession of Christ is not an isolated confession, but stands in a context from which it cannot be removed. This is also a *trinitarian* context. "The Son" is just as inseparably united with "the Father" as with "the Spirit"; yes, the confession of *Kyrios,* who is active

[6] On the relationship to the Old Testament, cf. Gustaf Wingren, *Skapelsen och lagen,* and Ragnar Bring, *Bibelns auktoritet och bibelns bruk* (Lund, 1958).

in the church, is at the same time a confession of the Spirit, *Pneuma*.

But even if the trinitarian perspective appears frequently in the New Testament, it is of utmost importance that it has been clearly formulated in the two classic documents of the church, in the threefold *Apostolicum* and *Nicaenum*. This trinitarian formulation permits the Christian confession to appear in all its wealth and fulness.

It is not our purpose here to analyze the confession of the ancient church in its entirety. We will restrict ourselves to "the second article," to the confession of Christ as formulated in the Nicene Creed and interpreted in the Chalcedonian formula. The emphasis is especially on the Incarnation. The confession of the Incarnation is in itself nothing new. The New Testament confession too was a confession of the Word which "became flesh and dwelt among us."

The confession of the ancient church as a whole is a defensive confession. It is formulated to serve as a foundation of faith. It originated at a time when serious struggles rocked the church and there was even danger that the Christian faith might be dissolved in a syncretistic chaos. Its chief purpose was to prevent this development. The question is to what extent the confession of the ancient church succeeded in preserving and developing the biblical confession. This question is concerned especially with Christology. Whoever comes from the New Testament to the christological debates and decisions by the councils of the ancient church cannot escape the feeling that he has entered into a different world. The terminology used in the debates is to a large extent taken from Greek thought. The Bible does not speak of how "the essence" of the Father and the Son are related to one another, nor of the relationship between the two "natures" of Christ. The very questions asked seem to have been different, and a purely theoretical speculation seems to have taken the place of soteriological orientation. The liberal theology of the nineteenth century pronounced severe judgments on the Christology of the ancient church. Recently an exegete of a different spirit, Oscar Cullmann, has also spoken out in criticism. His chief point of view is that New Testament Christology is thoroughly "func-

tional," while that of the ancient church is given to fruitless speculations about the relationship of the different "natures" to one
another. Such a problem, says Cullmann, is "Greek" rather than
"Jewish-biblical." Cullmann is thinking especially of the Chalcedonian formula. It is, of course, not at all strange that the
defenders of the Christian faith should employ conceptions taken
from the Greek world of thought in which they lived. This was
rather a compelling necessity which they must have regarded
as an indispensable condition of their work. If they had not
spoken the language of the times they would have condemned
themselves and the faith they wanted to defend to a fatal isolation.
This is one side of the matter. The other side is that here, as
always, such a transposition of the content of faith into a new
frame of reference is accompanied by obvious dangers.

The Nicene Creed may be regarded as an amplification of the
Apostles' Creed. Both of these occupy a unique position in Christianity. They command incomparably greater ecumenical acceptance than any other confessions. Almost all the churches of
Christendom have accepted them. The exceptions are few. Furthermore, all through the centuries they have been used in the
worship service and in the occasional services of the church. In
other words, they are not accepted simply as venerable historical
documents. They are confessions of faith which really function
as such, and thus prove themselves to be living confessions of
the church.

The trinitarian character of these two confessions is, as we
have said, in line with the witness of the New Testament. Just as
the confession of Christ was indissolubly connected with the confession of God as the God of creation, the law, and salvation, so
it was also inseparably connected with the confession of the Spirit
through whom *Christus Kyrios* continues his saving activity in
his church, i.e., to that Spirit which is the Holy Spirit of God
and of Christ. While the threefold confession provides a comprehensive expression of the content of the divine revelation, its
thrust at the same time is directed to what in various ways threatened to undermine and dissolve the Christian faith. This is true
of the *Apostolicum,* and still more of the *Nicaenum.* This is true,
also, of all three of the articles. The first article is directed against

Marcion's and Gnosticism's division of the conception of God by their denial of the identity between the God of creation and the God of redemption. The third article rejects an ecstatic and fanciful spiritualism, which, in a way, by separating the Spirit from Christ, uses the Spirit for its own purposes. Since, however, connection with Christ has not been directly expressed in the text accepted at the meeting in Constantinople, where it read simply that the Spirit "proceeds from the Father," it was found that the formula did not provide sufficient defense against the fanatical movements, and that it therefore needed to be complemented.[7] This was done, but unfortunately in different ways in the East and in the West. In the East the formulation was "proceedeth from the Father through the Son." In the West, however, it read "proceedeth from the Father and the Son." This disputed *filioque* contributed later to the separation between the East and the West.

The second article of the Nicene Creed was also formulated as a defense. The emphasis is on the Incarnation. The statements made here about Christ are designed to emphasize to the same degree his divinity and his humanity. The starting point of the confession is the New Testament confession of *Kyrios:* "We believe in one Lord Jesus Christ." The divinity of this Lord is established by a number of statements. These are meant to express the identity between God and Christ—"true God," "of one substance with the Father"—and also the relationship between them: Christ is "begotten of his Father," he is "God *of* God," "Light *of* light," etc. This one Lord "was incarnate" and "was made man."

These definitions are intended to reject two different false conceptions. On the one hand, they reject the idea that Christ was supposed to be only a human hero or an intermediary being between God and man, or a lower god. In opposition he is declared to be "of one substance with the Father," *homousios*. When in this connection they insert the statement about Christ's participation in creation—"by whom all things were made"—the intention is to affirm the inseparable unity between the God of creation

---

[7] Cf. George S. Hendry, *The Holy Spirit in Christian Theology* (Philadelphia: Westminster, 1956), pp. 37ff.

and the God of redemption. The thrust here as in the first article is against Marcionite and Gnostic attempts to separate the God of creation from the God of redemption and to make him a lower god. The God who becomes incarnate in Christ and through him carries out the work of redemption is no one else than the God of creation. On the other hand, the Nicene confession of Christ also rejects all tendencies to regard Christ as a kind of theophany or a divinity wandering around incognito on earth. The humanity of Christ is true humanity, not a kind of abstract humanity which the divine person put on as a covering cloak.

Finally it is important to note that the Nicene confession of Christ stands in a soteriological context. In affirming the Incarnation they say that *Christus-Kyrios* "for us men, and for our salvation, came down from heaven, And was incarnate." To make absolutely sure, this "for us" is repeated in connection with the cross: "and was crucified also for us under Pontius Pilate." These words show clearly that the statements about the person of Christ are not, so to speak, free speculation. What is stated about his person stands rather in an inseparable connection with his redemptive work. This connection is clearly recognized in the statements of the church fathers from Irenaeus to Athanasius. "Unless man had overcome the enemy of man, the enemy would not have been legitimately vanquished. And again, unless it had been God who had freely given salvation, we could never have possessed it securely. And unless man had been joined to God, he could never have become a partaker of incorruptibility." [8] Athanasius writes: "Just as we would not have been liberated from sin and the curse unless it had been truly human flesh which the Logos assumed, so also man could not have been made divine unless the incarnate Word were one with the Father in nature and were his own Word." [9]

We turn now to the Chalcedonian formula. The christological conflicts continued after Nicaea. The two conceptions against which the Nicene Creed had been directed continued under new forms. In this situation the Chalcedonian formula is intended to follow the Nicene line and to create a harmonious formula that

[8] Irenaeus, *Adversus haereses*, III, 18, 7.
[9] Athanasius, *Oratio contra arianos*, 2, 70.

would put an end to the christological conflicts. We note the following chief points in the decision of the council. Christ is "complete in Godhead and complete in manhood." He is "recognized in two natures, without confusion, without change, without division, without separation; the distinction of natures being in no way annulled by the union, but rather the characteristics of each nature being preserved and coming together to form one person and subsistence (*hypostasis*), not as parted or separated into two persons, but one and the same Son and Only-begotten God the Word, Lord Jesus Christ."

How is this interpretation of the Incarnation related to the biblical confession of Christ? Is Chalcedon a defense for it, or is it true that these formulations go astray and lead to "fruitless speculations"? Such a question cannot be answered by a simple and direct answer. First of all it is obvious that the terminology is not biblical but "Greek." They think in categories other than those of the biblical authors. But this does not necessarily mean that the problem on which they work and the answer they give were foreign to the biblical confession. Such a conclusion would be premature. If we are really to investigate the relationship between Chalcedon and the biblical confession of Christ, we must establish not only what Chalcedon positively maintains but also what it wants to reject as heresy. In its own words, the Chalcedonian formula wants to maintain that Christ is "complete in Godhead and complete in manhood." The meaning of these statements. appear most clearly through the lines of demarcation drawn by the famous and much-discussed definitive terms: "without confusion, without change, without division, without separation." The desire is to differentiate the confession of Christ, on the one hand, from a conception in which the divine more or less obliterates the human, and, on the other hand, from a conception that separates the divine from the human in such a way that Christ appears as an intermediary being between God and man. This twofold demarcation is unquestionably in line with the biblical confession of Christ. The first appears in the Bible itself, as the biblical authors struggle against a "Docetism" which denies that Christ "has come in the flesh," or, in other words, denies his true humanity. It is just as clear that the other line has a direct connection with the biblical confession of Christ, according to which *Christus-Kyrios* is the object of prayer, supplication, and divine homage. "The Word became flesh." It is God himself and not some intermediary being who has become incarnate in Christ and through him carries out the work of salvation.

The fact is, therefore, that Chalcedon not only was intended to be but also actually was a defense of the biblical confession of Christ. It is to a large degree a biblical problem that reappears in the christological work of the ancient church. The answer that is given is also centrally biblical. The Christology of the ancient church which we find here does not represent a "Hellenization" of the Christian faith, but rather a rejection of Hellenization. At the same time it is obvious that the form of the questions is Greek rather than biblical. The Bible does not speak about the relationship of the two natures of Christ, or in general of his "natures." This form of the question in the theology of the ancient church has led to great difficulties. It invited attempts to seek a rational solution, which in reality could not be produced. The Chalcedonian formula itself is the best evidence that a rational solution was impossible. It stops at the negative limitations: "without confusion, without change, without division, without separation." God and man must not be mixed together. God is God and man is man. At the same time the unity of the person of Christ must not be destroyed. These negations have sometimes been regarded as a failure. In reality they render a great service. That the formula stops with negations means, not that it encourages "speculations," but that it sets up a barrier against them. To do this was no doubt the chief purpose of the formula. How well it succeeded is a different question.

The question as to the significance of Chalcedon may be seen from various points of view. The purpose of Chalcedon was to give an answer to the christological question that would create unity and would become a firm basis for further christological thought. In this it was unsuccessful, since the formula did not end the struggle. The conflicts not only continued, but resulted in schisms, and separate churches were organized both of Monophysitic and Nestorian type. But this does not mean that Chalcedon was of slight importance. The fact is that there has hardly been a theological formula that has had such enormous influence. It became the foundation of christological thinking not only in the Eastern Orthodox church to the present time, but also in the West throughout the centuries. In the preceding we have seen how Congar, when he formulates his attitude to the Reformation, uses Chalcedon as a frame of reference in his argument. One evidence of its great influence within modern Roman theology is the enormous work in three volumes with a number of authors which has recently been published under the title, *Das Konzil von Chalkedon: Geschichte und Gegenwart* (1951-1954).

The Chalcedonian formula has therefore been very highly regarded and, at least in the greater part of Christendom, has been accepted as a foremost, authoritative, christological document. How it has functioned and to what extent its fundamental ideas have been accepted is another matter. The formula manifested two chief interests. It wanted to assure the due recognition of both the "divinity" and the "humanity" of Christ. At the same time it wanted to safeguard the unity and integrity of his person. That the formula enjoyed undisputed authority does not mean, however, that it has functioned effectively. A brief review of the development in the West will serve to illustrate how the matter stands.

In regard to the first set of problems we find *both* ideas which show how difficult it was to give due credit to Christ's true and concrete humanity, *and* movements which one-sidedly attach the Christian life to the sufferings which Christ endured as man. The first of these attitudes is characteristic of Scholastic theology. We have already noted previously what difficulties Thomas Aquinas had with those biblical statements which give frank expression to "the true humanity" of Jesus. According to Thomas "the human nature" of Christ contained a higher stratum which was unmoved by temptations, anxiety, and suffering.[10] On the other hand, the picture of the purely human suffering of Christ stands in the center of the form of piety that was dominant during the last part of the Middle Ages, and which stressed imitation of Christ and meditation upon his purely human sufferings (*imitatio et meditatio*

[10] Cf. above. p. 70.

108

passionis Christi). The emphasis was on sentimental compassion for the purely human pain that Jesus had to suffer.

It is not true at all, therefore, that the fundamental ideas of Chalcedon permeated and determined theology and piety in the West during the Middle Ages. Instead we find a struggle between two tendencies. In the one his divinity more or less eliminates his humanity, or at least does not give it an adequate place (or, in the words of Chalcedon, there is "a confusion of natures"). In the other we find tendencies in which the suffering human being becomes everything, with the result not only that the "divinity" of Christ is obscured, but also, because the cross becomes merely a martyr cross, that the conception of the victorious Christ is lost.

From what we have just said it is clear that not even the Chalcedonian formula was able to preserve the unity and integrity of the person of Christ in the succeeding periods of history. The question of how this could be must be examined also from another point of view: that of the work of redemption. The fact of the matter is that the unity of the person is inseparably connected with the unity of redemption. The Bible viewed redemption under two aspects: as an act done on behalf of man, and as an act of God. The fact that it saw redemption under these two aspects did not in any sense dissolve the unity. When we come to Chalcedon, it may almost appear as if here the person of Christ was treated in isolation from his redemptive work. This is, however, only apparently so. In Chalcedon as well as in the Nicene Creed there is a direct connection between what is said about the person of Christ and the understanding of his redemptive work. If the person is a unity, "without division, without separation," so also is his work. The foundation of Chalcedonian Christology is the conception of salvation in the ancient church which conceived of the work of Christ as at the same time a human and a divine act. An indication of this unity is the fact that here as in the Bible the cross and the resurrection stand in an indissoluble union. The act of Christ is at the same time a sacrificial and a victorious act. When we come to Scholasticism this two-sided unity is lost. Anselm's theory of the Atonement bears witness to this fact. In his theory it is not a unitary act seen under two aspects. Instead the work of salvation is split and divided into what Christ does as man (*qua homo*) and what he does as God (*qua deus*). In contrast to what Chalcedon advocated, both the person and the work are now "divided and separated."

We have shown how in various ways ideas have appeared which stand in conflict with the affirmations of Chalcedon. In spite of its authoritative position Chalcedon was not able to hinder this development. It would, of course, be wrong to blame Chalcedon for this development which was dependent on many different factors. But at the same time it may be said that the inadequate terms Chalcedon used *to some extent* tended to weaken its effectiveness. The use of the terms "two natures" could easily cause a split in the unity and integrity of the person which the formula was intended to maintain. But on the other hand, the fact that the formula was not able to do *everything* it was intended to do, cannot mean that its significance was small or unimportant. But we would be especially far wrong if we were to interpret the Christology of the ancient church, expressed in the Nicene Creed and further developed in the Chalcedonian formula, as a departure from the biblical confession of Christ. It was not only intended to be, it really was a defense of this confession, and by its concentration on the Incarnation it prevented the original Christian confession from being dissolved into syncretistic mist. The confession of the ancient church is not different from the original confession, but is the same confession in a different dress. The boundary lines Chalcedon drew up are in reality still very important guides. It is not surprising that ecumenical discussions often revert to the Chalcedon formula. Stephen Neill is correct when he writes in *The Ecumenical Review* that, according to his conviction, no Christology "which goes outside of the boundaries drawn up by Chalcedon will in the last analysis prove adequate." [11] We need only add that this does not mean that we are compelled to use the terminology of Chalcedon.

12. *THE THREE ARE ONE*

We will close this chapter with an investigation of how the Reformation confession is related to the two earlier confessions of Christ, the biblical and that of the ancient church. It is con-

[11] *The Ecumenical Review,* 1957, p. 200.

venient to begin with the confession of the ancient church with its center in the Incarnation.

It might seem at first that the formula "justification by faith alone" is not a direct confession of Christ. But, as we have seen, it is in a very real sense a confession of Christ. The word justification declares that someone is justified. Who justifies? The answer is, Christ. Where does he do this? Answer: in his church. Justification by faith alone is identical with "being made righteous," "being in fellowship with God," "forgiveness of sins, life, and salvation" through Christ alone, or through God's active *agape* alone. Justification by faith alone is a confession of the Christ who is active in his church and of the work he carries on in the church, as he—the risen and living Lord—carries out and realizes that redemptive work which he fulfilled on the cross during his days here on earth.

This view of "justification" is directed toward two fronts: in part against a doctrine of salvation with moralistic features, and in part against the spiritualism of the "fanatics." In both cases the thrust is directed against the idea that the basis of justification could be anything else than God's work of salvation which Christ carries on in his church through Word and Sacrament. When the Reformation opposes "righteousness of the law" and "work-righteousness," and thereby also the idea that human activity and "merits" could "contribute" to salvation, this is nothing else than the negation which follows directly on the positive statement that justification rests on Christ's redemptive act alone. The same is true about the polemic against the "fanatics." When the Spirit is separated from the Christ who is active in Word and Sacrament, the idea of human merit returns from a different direction.

This view of the redemptive work of Christ is inseparably connected with the confession of the ancient church to the Incarnation. When the Reformers accepted the confessional formulas of the ancient church in their confessional writings, the reason was not only that they wanted to emphasize their connection with the universal, "catholic" church. It was a matter of principle. A few words from Luther's exegesis of Galatians 1:3 in the large Commentary on Galatians will show this very clearly. "There-

111

fore mark this well that in the matter of justification, where we have to do with the overcoming of law, sin, death, devil, and all other evils, we must know no other God, but this God revealed and incarnate in the flesh."

The claim has sometimes been made that the Christology of the Reformation is an atonement Christology in contrast to the incarnation Christology of the ancient church, but this claim is without any foundation. The real situation is that Incarnation and Atonement are not separated, but constitute a unity. The Incarnation is not merely a presupposition for the later act of the Atonement. Rather the Atonement is, so to speak, included in the Incarnation, because the Incarnation means that Christ assumes the conditions of human life and takes upon himself the distress and curse that rests upon humanity.

That the Atonement is seen in this way, as tied together with the Incarnation, is related to the fact that the confession of the ancient church has been set free from the strait jacket of its Greek terminology. Luther frequently made critical statements about speculations concerning the two "natures" of Christ. These speculations are nothing but "sophistic" knowledge of Christ. Christ, he says, is not Christ because he has two natures. He has this "glorious and comforting name by virtue of his office and his work which he has assumed. That he is by nature man and God belongs to his own person. But that he uses his office and pours out his love and becomes my Savior and Redeemer, is all for my comfort and consolation." The point of view is soteriological-functional. The dominant question is no longer the contrast between divine and human nature, but, as the words quoted from his Commentary on Galatians clearly show, the antithesis between the power of God and the power of evil, between God's love and that which opposes his love. "The emphasis is not on a combination of the divine and the human natures. The decisive points in his thinking are not two substances set over against each other, but God's righteousness and the unrighteousness which rules in human life and results in the curse." [12]

The relation between the Reformation and the ancient church may be elucidated further by an examination of Congar's discus-

[12] Ragnar Bring, *Kristendomstolkningar* (Lund, 1950), p. 134.

sion of this subject. Congar has very rightly emphasized that the Reformation Christology is soteriological, and the Christology of the ancient church ontological. He has also rightly pointed out that the point of view of the Reformation agrees with "Semitic, prophetic, and biblical thinking rather than Greek." Nevertheless he seems to hold that the Greek conception of the ancient church provided a richer and, so to speak, more effective view than that of the Reformation. He makes the following statement. "Through the incarnation and after the incarnation God gives himself to us not only through his word, but really, and, as the ancient fathers said, substantially." The argument is that the Reformation does not give due recognition to the Incarnation.

Congar's reasoning rests on the presupposition that salvation as "participation in God's nature" is preferable to salvation as participation in God's *agape*. Such a conception stands in evident contrast to Luther's words in this matter. But the reason is not that God's *agape* is something secondary to God's "nature." On the contrary, to Luther God's "essence" or "nature" is identical with his *agape*. "In God's court and castle," he says, "is nothing but love." God's essence is precisely the love with which he gives himself to us. We may quote a very impressive statement about this matter. In a sermon on John 4:16ff., he writes: "Love is the one, eternal, unspeakable good and the most precious treasure, which is really God himself. From him everything comes, in him everything originates, and in and through this same love everything consists. Whoever remains in that love, remains in God and God in him, so that he and God become one loaf." [13] Such a statement, which speaks about "justification" as fellowship with God in terms that cannot be surpassed, shows that salvation as "participation in God's nature" cannot reasonably be regarded as a statement superior to what the Reformation means by talking about salvation as a fellowship and participation in God's *agape*. To be sure, Congar is right in claiming that an exclusive emphasis on justification as a forensic act tends to impoverish the conception of the Christian relationship to God as this was understood in the Bible and in the ancient church. It is obvious that such a one-sided emphasis has been found in the churches of the Refor-

[13] Luther, *EA* 19, 153-54.

mation, but it is equally obvious that this emphasis does not correspond to what the Reformation really said and intended. Instead, this interpretation is contrary, not only to the words of Luther just quoted, but to thousands of other passages and to the fundamental point of view which is expressed everywhere, and which has found its most classic formulation in the words of the *Small Catechism* about the union of forgiveness of sins, life, and salvation.

Against the background of this discussion we can deal with Congar's objection that the Incarnation has been neglected. This is really far from the truth because in the Reformation everything depends on the fact that in the Word and the sacraments Christ continues and actualizes the redemptive work he perfected during the days of his flesh. The Incarnation is not simply an isolated event which now belongs to the past. It is rather something which *continually functions,* and which now in the present is connected with the Word and the sacraments. In this respect there is no difference between Congar's view and that of the Reformation. There is no doubt a difference between them, but this difference is concerned with the relationship of the Incarnation to "the ministerial office." This is a question which we will discuss in a later chapter.

The import of what we have just said is that the conception of salvation as a participation in the divine "nature" can hardly be said to add anything to or make more profound the view of salvation perceiving everything as dependent on God's *agape,* which comes to us in Christ with life of God's life. On the contrary, it cannot be denied that the "ontological" conception, which accentuates salvation as participation in God's "substance," contains certain obvious dangers, of which we note especially two. One of these is the danger that the idea of substance can result in a division of Christ's one work of redemption. It is significant that Congar, who of course holds that the Reformation obscured Christ's humanity, maintains to the contrary that the humanity of Christ nevertheless had "a secondary" significance for salvation. The Reformation rejects in principle such a division. The redemptive work is one and indivisible. From one point of view it is altogether a human work, and from another point of view it is completely a divine act. The other danger in this conception of substance is that it opens the door to a "synergistic" interpretation of salvation. The reason for this is that the point of reference is the antithesis between divine and human nature, not, as in the Bible and in the Reformation, the conflict between God and the enemies opposed to him. On the basis of the first antithesis it is easy to conceive of Christ's human activity in salvation in a "synergistic" manner. His divine and his human activity stand over against one another in such a way that they limit and complement one another. Under these circumstances as soon as his human activity is emphasized, the result is that salvation is no longer fully and completely "from God." On the contrary, if the point of reference is the antithesis between God's will and the will hostile to him, these difficulties disappear in principle. If justification is by grace alone, it is impossible to divide the work of salvation as partly the work of God and partly the work of man in such a way that they balance one another. When from this point of view we speak about faith as receiving, about the venture of faith, the Yes of faith and the obedience of faith, this in no sense means that salvation is any less God's work and God's gift. "By grace alone" does not stand in opposition to human "activity," but to the acquiring of human merits. The reason for this is that the decisive contrast is not between God and man, but between God and "the destructive powers." There is no fear of talking about human "activity" or about man as God's "fellow worker." But this does not mean that faith is to be understood as a characteristic which qualifies man for salvation. Faith means that man is incorporated into that divine activity where man through Christ receives the righteousness of *God*. As we have said several times, and never tire of saying, justification by faith alone is identical with justification through Christ alone.

In the Reformation we encounter an evident attempt to set the Christology of the ancient church free from its inadequate terminology and conceptions. This is an evidence of the Reformation's strongly biblical orientation. The Reformation confession, like that of the ancient church, is a defense of the biblical confession of Christ. Its biblical character is obvious and unquestionable. But is not its interpretation of the Bible nevertheless one-sided? This is a question which we have already asked several times.

If we take note of the contemporary discussion about the Reformation, we will find that this question has two aspects. First of all it is concerned with the Reformation confession itself as this is expressed in the formula, "justification by faith alone." Does not this formula represent an exclusive Paulinism, or, over and above that, a one-sided and warped Paulinism? The other aspect is connected with the biblical view of the church as this is interpreted in modern exegetical research, which strongly emphasizes that the church from the very beginning appeared with a comparatively strong organization. The one-sidedness of the Reformation would then appear in the fact that it did not see clearly the significance which the organization and especially the "ministerial office," *ordo,* has in the New Testament conception. This question will be discussed in a later chapter. Here we confine ourselves to the question of the relationship of the Reformation confession to the Bible.

We must first consider somewhat this concept of one-sidedness. In the nature of the case a defensive confession has to be to some extent "one-sided." Its purpose is to reject certain definite misinterpretations and distorted conceptions. The controversial situation leads inevitably to a concentration on what is denied and to what in contrast is affirmed. If in this connection we speak about one-sidedness, it is a one-sidedness that is due to the concrete, historical situation. The situation is such that certain points of view must be advocated strenuously, or "one-sidedly." But this is not to say that one-sidedness needs to affect the nature of the matter at hand; or, in other words, that one distorted conception must be replaced with another.

The formula itself, "justification by faith alone," is evidently connected with such Pauline passages as Romans 1:17; 3:26; 5:1. But the word *alone* does not occur in any one of these. The question might be asked whether the Reformation in adopting this addition has not really tried to outdo Paul. This would certainly be the case if faith were understood here as an achievement through which man qualified himself for salvation. Yes, in that case they would not only have gone beyond Paul, but would have entered upon an entirely different way. As we have already seen, the meaning of the formula is very different: "by faith alone" is the same as "through Christ alone" and "through God's *agape* alone." In this meaning the formula agrees not only with Paul, but with the whole New Testament. The formulation is in line with Paul, but the content is not something specifically Pauline, but rather something common to all New Testament preaching. It is a concentrated expression for the gospel and good news the New Testament proclaims. It would be quite wrong to underestimate the significance of Paul's letters for the Reformation, but it would be just as wrong to characterize the Reformation as a one-sided Paulinism. When the Reformation and Paulinism are compared, it is natural enough to point out that both struggled against "the righteousness that is by the law," or "of works," and that in this respect the background is the same. This similarity cannot be denied. But two things must be taken into consideration here. In the first place, similarity is not the same as identity. Luther's situation was not the same as Paul's. In the second place, we find this opposition, not only in Paul, but in different form also in the Synoptic Gospels and in the Johannine writings, and in the New Testament in general. The reason for this is that the gospel proclaimed is a gospel about God's act in Christ, or a gospel of salvation "through Christ alone." The statement, "There is salvation in no one else" (Acts 4:12), is the kernel of the whole New Testament proclamation. It is this central biblical message and nothing else which sounds forth fully and clearly in the preaching of the Reformation. To be sure, it has its own peculiar tone, just as Paul, John, and the Synoptic Gospels each have theirs. But the time is past when "liberal" theology could set up Paul against what they called "the simple teaching of Jesus." Modern biblical study in no sense minimizes the differences between biblical authors. The New Testament is not a uniform *doctrina*. But neither is it a collection of various disparate parts. Everything is tied together by the uniform message, the kerygma of God's redemptive act in and through Christ, which is altogether a work "of grace" and of God's *agape,* and which can be received only in faith. In the light of this insight the Reformation confession appears clearly and unequivocally as a legitimate continuation and interpretation of the biblical conception as a whole.

117

But even though all this is very clear, it is just as apparent that the Reformation confession has not always furnished effective protection for what it wanted to maintain and preserve. The long accounts of the inner conflicts which appeared quickly in the time after the Reformation show how difficult it was for the Reformation confession to perform its guardian work. The history of this period manifests a certain obvious analogy to the history following Nicaea and Chalcedon. Just as the confession of the ancient church was misinterpreted in various ways, so it happened, too, with that of the Reformation. Many of the objections we have noted previously are in reality concerned with these misinterpretations. Many of these found apparent support in some of the radical statements of Luther, who certainly did not weigh his words very carefully. Misinterpretations have arisen because these statements have been isolated and made the object of absurd logical deductions. Other misinterpretations have appeared because the Reformation confession has been approached from presuppositions and problems that were foreign to it. This is the case, for instance, when the will of God and the will of man are conceived of as standing in a logical, complementary relationship, with the result that what happens in salvation has to be divided between what God does and what man does. When the attempt is made to maintain the Reformation view of salvation on the basis of this presupposition, the result is an inescapable dilemma. On the one hand, the desire is to reduce, in a way foreign to the Reformation, the activity of man to the least possible amount; and on the other hand, this least amount means that faith is regarded as an achievement qualifying man for salvation.

Misinterpretation of this sort, which arises from a schematic isolation and abstract logical deduction, is quite common. We may mention two examples. We find it when the forensic aspect of justification is isolated. This means that the central thought of the Reformation as to how Christ deals with man here in his church and incorporates him into a living fellowship with himself is not given due recognition. The result is that the inseparable connection between justification and sanctification is lost. Another variant of this type of misunderstanding is found in the tendency appearing here and there to isolate faith from "works."

The most grotesque example of such abstract logical deduction is found in the statement that good works are harmful to salvation.

These examples will have to suffice. We will not make any attempt to explicate how the various theological movements and types of piety have reacted to the central confession of the Reformation through the centuries. It would take us too far afield if we were to analyze how the heritage of the Reformation meets us in the period of Orthodoxy in an intellectualized and so to speak rigid form; how in Pietism the Reformation motifs contend with subjectivism and individualism; how the Enlightenment, in spite of its appeal to the Reformation as "a pioneer," is with its moralism in reality quite foreign to the fundamental religious conception of the Reformation; and then go on through the variegated nineteenth century down to our own time, in which at any rate we do find earnest attempts to revive and set free what was essential in the confession of the Reformation—without apotheosizing either the Reformation or Luther.

But if we must refrain here from writing post-Reformation history, it may be in place to say a few words about the perspective which can and ought to be imposed on this highly variegated history, as also in general on the history of Christian thought and piety. It is just as impossible to use the category of evolutionary development as it is to differentiate schematically various periods with the help of such categories as purity and apostasy. Neither of these points of view do justice to the actual historical development. The one, developed in terms of evolution, becomes guilty of a false idealism. It is by no means true that Christian history could be characterized as a development toward greater purity and clarity. But neither is it true that Christian history could be depicted by a schematic and stereotyped division into periods, where periods of faithfulness to the gospel are differentiated from periods of apostasy. The only legitimate perspective is the *dramatic*. What actually happens in the course of time is that the gospel finds itself in a continual struggle in order to guard itself against corruptions. These corruptions may appear in what may seem entirely different forms in different times, but in reality there is a far greater similarity between them than is apparent at first sight. No period in the history of Christianity has escaped this struggle, nor can any period without further ado be characterized as apostate. The New Testament shows quite clearly how even in the early church there was a severe struggle for the purity of the gospel. The Middle Ages have been severely criticized, not only by Protestants, but also, as we have seen, by Roman theologians. But this does not mean that this period with its deep piety could be spoken of as "a dark night." This is not at all true. Even if we may find in the writings of the Reformation biased critical judgments, nevertheless the relationship of the Reformation to the Middle Ages is in no sense simply negative.

If we apply a dramatic perspective to the history of Christianity, the position and the significance of the confessions of both the ancient church and the Reformation appear in clearer light. Both are the evidence of the struggle of the gospel itself against corruptions of its message. That they were not able as such to prevent corruptions and aberrations of different kinds is quite understandable in the light of this perspective. But this does not nullify their significance. Their importance lies not simply in the fact that they are historical documents of the greatest order, but also and especially in the fact that they continue to be active factors in the life of the church. It is hardly possible to overestimate the significance of the fact that the Apostles' and the Nicene Creeds have become permanent parts in the liturgical service. Their position in worship life makes them perpetually living confessions. The Reformation confession, to be sure, has not found a place in the same way in the worship life of the Reformation churches. But it has nevertheless to a large extent put its stamp on worship life not only in preaching but also in the liturgy. We must also remember the tremendous part the hymns of the Reformation have played as an expression of the confession, and also the influence that a document like that of the *Small Catechism* has had. In general it must be emphasized that we have been too ready to think of the history of Christianity from the point of view of the professional development of theology. Theology has indeed played a very important part. But it must at the same time be pointed out that worship life manifests a *relatively* independent attitude toward theology. This fact must be taken into account if we are to arrive at an objec-

120

tive and correct conception of the significance both these confessions had for the life of the church.

It is true, of course, that the Reformation confession does not enjoy such universal recognition as the confession of the ancient church. It is the confession of only a part of Christendom, and, as *Tridentinum* affirms, a confession whose legitimacy is questioned. It may seem presumptuous, therefore, to try to designate it as one of the principal Christian confessions. Nevertheless if we dare claim this distinction for it, we can do so only on the basis that it stands in positive agreement with the confession of the ancient church and especially with that of the New Testament. It may be claimed, however, that the Reformation confession is on its way to acceptance by a larger constituency. Evidence of this may be found in the modern ecumenical discussions. At the conference in Edinburgh (1937) there were many questions discussed about which different opinions were expressed. The only question on which the conference made a unanimous statement was "The Grace of our Lord Jesus Christ." This report says in part: "God in his free outgoing love justifies and sanctifies us through Christ, and his grace thus manifested is appropriated by faith, which itself is a gift of God. Justification and sanctification are two inseparable aspects of God's gracious action in dealing with sinful man." [14] This statement was accepted by the Orthodox delegates as well as by all others and without doubt expresses what was the greatest concern of the Reformation. We saw previously that there has been some change in the attitude of Roman theologians, but these changes do not mean that all criticism has ceased. These changes show, however, that the criticism has changed so that the object is no longer the total conception of the Reformation but rather those "negations" which are said to be connected with its valuable—and in the contemporary situation necessary—positive intentions. Recognition is accompanied by a rather sharp criticism of the conditions prevailing in the church at the close of the Middle Ages. These conditions contained much that was contrary to "good Catholic" tradition, a tradition which is in basic agreement with the positive intentions of the Reformation.

[14] *Edinburgh, 1937*, p. 224.

Even if this second declaration contains many complicated problems, there is no reason to criticize the fact that they seek to present and emphasize those aspects in earlier history which agree with the confession of the Reformation.

We have now considered the three confessions of Christ which we have designated as the three chief confessions of Christendom: the original, fundamental biblical confession and the two later "defensive" confessions. These three not only stand in a close connection, but are in reality *one*. They are all confessions of Christ as *Kyrios*. *Kyrios* is the chief word of the confession of the early church. It is also the chief word in the Nicene Creed, as is indicated by the opening words of the second article, "I believe in one Lord Jesus Christ." The same is true of the Reformation confession. "Justification by faith alone" is a confession of the Lord who actualizes his redemptive work in his church. *Kyrios* is furthermore the chief word in Luther's explanation of the second article: "I believe that Jesus Christ . . . is my Lord." The confessions of the ancient church and of the Reformation both use "the apostolic key" in their interpretation of the message of holy Scripture.

According to all three of these confessions the work of redemption is performed by a man in history, but it is at the same time God's own work. This fact emphasizes the connection between the second and the first article: the God of redemption is none other than the God of creation. With its chief formula, *"sola fide," "sola gratia,"* "through Christ alone," the Reformation confession has its central point in that which continually takes place in the church of Christ, where the crucified, risen, and living Lord "justifies." In this way it emphasizes the connection between the second and the third article, between the work of Christ and the work of the Spirit. These differences in emphasis are due to the differences in the historical situation, and are determined by what is required for the defense in each case. But this does not mean that the confessions have a different content. The confession of Christ is the same as it was from the beginning. In reality it is not a question of three different confessions, but of one and the same fundamental Christian confession. The three are one.

CHAPTER 4

TRADITION

13. *SCRIPTURE AND TRADITION*

As in the preceding chapters we listened to Roman theologians, we found how anxious they are that the word of the Bible shall find its proper place in the life of the church. They recognized what the Reformation was able to do in this respect at a time when the biblical Word to a large extent had been thrust aside by "decadent Scholasticism" and legends. They deplored the fact that for a long time the Council of Trent contributed to the weakening of the position of the Bible in the church. They spoke in favor of a biblical renaissance in their church. We will listen to yet another testimony to the serious concern that the biblical Word shall really receive that place in the church which it ought to have. I refer to Divo Barsotti's book already mentioned, *Il mistero christiano e la parola di Dio* ("The Christian Mystery and the Word of God") (1953).

The title suggests the chief purpose of the author. He wants to demonstrate the inseparable connection between "the mystery" of the Lord's Supper and the biblical Word of God. Without this connection with the Word of God the mystery of salvation offered in the Sacrament would be hidden. The Sacrament would then no longer be a sacrament. Barsotti speaks in the most forceful terms of what the biblical Word of God means for the life of the church. The divine revelation was completed with the Incarnation of the Word. But the function of Holy Scripture is to be an extension of the Incarnation in the life of the church. God's activity in the church depends on the Word of God in Scripture. The biblical Word which we encounter in the worship service, through "the mouth" of the church, is a living, creative, and effective Word of God. It is "the word of one who speaks," and this one is God. This Word of God addresses itself to each one directly and personally. It is, as Barsotti frequently says, "a word to you." The mystery of the divine Word reveals itself to him who lives in the church and "listens." The biblical Word becomes a word from the lips of Jesus and not merely a historical document. That it becomes a living Word of God in the present depends on Jesus' presence in his church. *He* prevents it from becoming merely a historical, human document.[1] Thus the Word of God becomes the bearer of "a special grace" (*una grazia speciale*). It remains powerful. It "has the power to heal the sick, just as it did when Jesus spoke it; it has power to drive away the demons, to convert sinners, to give peace to anxious souls, to save in desperate situations, and to be an effective means against all the powers of evil." [2]

This presentation speaks, as we see, not only of the inseparable connection between the Word of God and the Sacrament but also directly about the Word as "a means of grace." He who belongs in the Reformation tradition finds here ideas with which he is well acquainted. It is possible that Barsotti's words about "the extension" of the incarnate Word through the Word active in the church will appear to him strange, and the same may be true of the statement that the "mystery" of the divine Word is unveiled in the fellowship of the church. If so, it is due to the fact that he is accustomed to using other formulations. In reality we meet here ideas that were central and indispensable in the preaching of the Reformation: that Christ is living and active in the Word, that in the church of Christ the Spirit makes the Word appear as the living power it really is, and thus unveils the secret which is nothing else than God's incomprehensible and saving love. When this happens, the Bible is no longer a human, historical document. Then its message makes itself felt as a living and active word of God, which is "the power of God for salvation to every one who has faith" (Rom. 1:16). The church proclaims the living Word of God, and this Word reveals its power in the fellowship of the church.

[1] Barsotti, *Il mistero christiano e la parola di Dio*, pp. 175ff.
[2] *Ibid.*, p. 274.

In examining the attitude of the Reformation to the Scriptures, we must stress to begin with that the characteristic feature of the Reformation is not that it maintains Scripture as a formal authority. For a long time it has been customary to characterize the Reformation by speaking about its two "principles": the so-called material principle, *sola fide,* and the formal principle, *sola scriptura.* It is undeniable that the Reformation appealed to the Scriptures as final authority. Such an appeal to Scripture, however, is not at all something new. The Christian church has done so from the very beginning. The Bible to which the apostolic proclamation appealed was the Old Testament. The apostles wanted to incorporate the work of Christ into that context of divine activity to which the Old Testament bore witness, and to understand Christ and his work as the fulfilment of the promises of God which had been given in the days of the "old covenant." By establishing the canon of the New Testament the young church wanted to preserve the apostolic message of Christ intact. That the New Testament together with the Old Testament became a "canon" meant that Scripture as a whole was established as the guide for the proclamation of the Christian church.

The appeal to the authority of Scripture on the part of the Reformation was therefore in line with the constant practice of the Christian church through the centuries. Neither was such a formulation as *sola scriptura* something new. We find this also in the great teacher of the Middle Ages, Thomas Aquinas. The term "canonicity," he says, means that Scripture is the rule and guide for the teaching of the church. The canonical Scriptures alone determine the content of faith (*sola scriptura est regula fidei*). Scripture includes the whole truth necessary for salvation. The successors of the apostles are bound by this. They cannot introduce something new beyond that which has been given by the apostles. As successors to the apostles, says Thomas, the bishops are trustworthy only to the extent that their proclamation agrees with Scripture (*in quantum nobis anunciant ea quae illi in scriptis relinquerunt*).[3] Neither did the theology of the later Middle Ages make any change in this respect. Nominalistic theology wanted instead to strengthen this emphasis on the au-

[3] P. E. Persson, *Sacra doctrina,* pp. 54, 66.

thority of Scripture by reinforcing it with a theory of inspiration. Later on, as is quite well known, post-Reformation Orthodoxy became very interested in establishing a theory of the inspiration of Scripture which would testify to its formal authority and to its character as in every respect an infallible, divine document. But such questions about formal authority did not greatly interest the Reformers, at any rate not Luther. Their interest in Scripture had an entirely different frame of reference.

If we are to determine what the significance of Scripture was for the Reformation, two points of view appear in the foreground. In the first place, the Reformation returned the Bible to its central place in the life of the church. This was due to its clear conception of the Word as a means of grace. If in this connection the Reformers appealed not only to the biblical Word as such, but also laid much stress on the spoken Word, this in no sense meant a minimizing of the position of the Bible. There is no competition between the written and the spoken Word. The proclamation is altogether a proclamation of the biblical Word and the biblical message.

In the second place, the Reformation approached the Bible with "the apostolic key." It is often said that the Reformation used "justification by faith alone" as a divining rod in its interpretation of Scripture. This may very well be said. But it would be wrong to claim that the Reformation has discovered or put together a new key to the treasure of Scripture. If we let the Reformation formula be what it is, namely, a statement about the work of salvation which the living Christ, *Kyrios,* performs in his church, it becomes apparent at once that there can be no question about a "new" key. The key used is none other than the apostolic *Kyrios* key. For Luther's view of Scripture and its interpretation it is highly significant that again and again he points to the way Scripture "preaches Christ," and the fact that Christ is "the star and kernel" of Scripture, Scripture's Lord—*Kyrios.* Scripture can be rightly understood only from this point of view. An interpretation of Scripture that does not use this *Kyrios* key is a corruption.

This means further that Scripture is its own interpreter, and that its message is self-evident. When post-Reformation Orthodoxy speaks of Scripture as its own interpreter (*sui ipsius interpres*), and as self-evident (*per se evidens*), it expresses points of view which not only may be found in the writings of the Reformation but are also of fundamental importance. An interpretation of Scripture through the *Kyrios* key is not an interpretation from without, nor is it an interpretation read into the Scriptures. In reality it expresses the view of the New Testament itself when it is read in this context. The apostolic message of the New Testament is concentrated around the confession of Christ as *Kyrios*. It is this confession which reveals the purpose of the acts of God recorded in the Old Testament.

The reference to Christ as the *Kyrios* of Scripture does not mean therefore that the Reformation is concerned only with those biblical writings that deal directly with Christ, or, in other words, the New Testament. Nor does it mean that the Old Testament is taken into account only insofar as its statements may be interpreted as referring to Christ, or to the extent that the Old Testament is quoted in the New. The Old Testament has its own word to speak.[4] The decisive point is that Christ stands in the context of the whole sequence of divine acts from the creation and the fall to the final consummation, about which the Bible bears witness from first to last. In this comprehensive history of God's dealings with the world and humanity Christ is the mid-point as the one through whom God realizes his creative and redemptive will, and thereby he stands as the Lord of Scripture. Everything hinges on Scripture being interpreted on the basis of this central message. In this context we must understand the warning frequently uttered by the Reformation and especially by Luther against permitting the interpretation of Scripture to become dependent on other presuppositions than those of Scripture itself, as the Scholastics did, and especially against a philosophical viewpoint dependent on Aristotle.

In reference to the Reformation it must be especially emphasized that it is concerned with the testimony of Scripture *as a whole*. This does not in any way militate against some well-known and often-quoted words of Luther to the effect that, if his opponents quote Scripture against Christ, he will quote Christ

[4] Wingren, *Skapelsen och lagen*, pp. 17ff.

against Scripture. It is not Luther's meaning that there actually could be a conflict between Scripture and Christ. His radical formulation is directed against those Scholastic or fanciful allegorical interpretations which do not properly set forth the real content of Scripture. Nor does he mean that the *Kyrios* key may be used to segregate certain passages of Scripture as being human and historically conditioned from what has the character of the Word of God and is therefore of permanent value. Such an attitude is completely foreign to the Reformation's view of the Bible. This view speaks at the same time of Christ as the Lord of Scripture and of the testimony Scripture as a whole presents.

It was from this starting point—the interpretation of Scripture as revolving about the message of Christ—that the Reformation set forth its criticism of certain factors in the contemporary life of the church, in the "tradition" which expressed itself there in teaching and practice. The testimony of Scripture had to have validity over against what had been prescribed and taught by ecclesiastical authorities, insofar as their teaching was found to be contrary to the gospel about God's redemptive act in Christ. Again, this appeal of the Reformation to Scripture against ecclesiastical authorities was not something new. The opposition movements during the Middle Ages had done this too, when they demanded reforms within the church in various respects. But the difference between these and the Reformation was that they did not have the same clear and sure foundation in the biblical message as did the Reformation. It was precisely because the interest of the Reformation was so completely positive, and because it wanted nothing else than to "put the gospel on the lampstand," that its criticisms struck so much deeper. The result was that the question of the relationship between the authority of Scripture and of "tradition" acquired a relevance which it had not had earlier. If we go back to Thomas Aquinas, we find that the relationship between Scripture and the tradition represented by the church organization of Pope and councils is conceived of in a very unsophisticated sense. Thomas combines his heavy emphasis on the normative character of Scripture with a conviction that the church's teaching ministry provides the correct interpretation of Scripture and thus leads the "tradition" on the right way. Thomas of course grants that false conceptions of faith may arise. When this happens, Pope and councils must provide the true interpretation of the content of faith. He does not reckon with the possibility that these agencies could be wrong. He assumes rather that there is full agreement between Scripture and the decisions arrived at by the leadership of the church. These decisions are regarded as a continuing interpretation of Scripture through the years.[5]

When the Reformation leveled its criticism against church practices authorized by the hierarchy, and thereby questioned the privilege of ecclesiastical leadership to provide an infallible interpretation of Scripture, the earlier "unsophisticated" conception of the relationship between Scripture and tradition could no longer be maintained. Rome was forced to define its stand more clearly. The Council of Trent supplied this definition. Since the decision of the Council spoke of the authority which Scripture *and* tradition possess, subsequent centuries took this to mean that these two authorities were set side by side as equals. In the preceding we saw that this interpretation of the meaning of the decision is disputed by modern Roman theologians. The correct interpretation should be that Scripture provides the revealed truth of the gospel and tradition provides an authoritative interpretation of it. We have seen that in modern Roman theology there is a conscious attempt to emphasize more strongly the central position of Scripture and its significance for the life of the church. They frankly concede that during the latter Middle Ages the Bible had not been given its proper place. They also acknowledge fully the desire of the Reformation to place the Bible in the center, and they regret that the opposition to the Reformation, as expressed in the decisions of the Council of Trent, caused the Roman church for a long time to take an unfortunate negative attitude to the Bible and to its distribution and use. Such a presentation as that by Congar indicates clearly how they struggle with this problem of the relationship between Scripture and tradition. He wants to find a solution which would give a proper place to the authority of Scripture and at the same time maintain the authority which belongs to the *magis-*

[5] Persson, *Sacra doctrina,* p. 71.

terium of the church. The following formulation is characteristic: We must refer to tradition as a whole, but within this tradition the Scriptures are the objective and normative rule. The *magisterium* of the church does not judge Scripture, but only Scripture's interpretation by the faithful.

We return now to the Reformation. Just as Thomas' *sola scriptura* did not involve a negative attitude to "tradition," the same is true also of the Reformation. Its positive attitude is well attested both in principle and in practice. The most forceful expression of this attitude appears in the chief confession of the Reformation, the Augsburg Confession. Here it is declared that "There is nothing here [in the Confession] that departs from the Scriptures or the church catholic, or the church of Rome in so far as the ancient church is known to us from its writers." It also declares that "the dissension is concerned with a certain few abuses which have crept into the church without proper authority." It has been said that these formulations were made in view of the proposed conference, and that these statements therefore were given a conciliatory tone as far as possible. This is no doubt true. It is equally true that Luther would have preferred sharper language. This statement that it was a question of eliminating "certain abuses" certainly gives no indication of what actually took place. But from this we must not draw the conclusion that Luther manifested a more negative attitude to tradition. Historical writing which seeks to make Melanchthon the traditionalist and Luther an anti-traditionalist has no basis in fact. Luther, too, was anxious to emphasize continuity especially with the ancient church and the church fathers, to whose writings he frequently appealed. In reality it may be said rather that in a formal sense Melanchthon seems to be more attached to the tradition, but as regards the matter itself Luther has nevertheless a stronger inner affinity with the conception of the ancient church, with the historical perspective of salvation which was dominant among the church fathers as they—to use Luther's words—conceived of Christ as "the victor over sin, death, and eternal damnation."

Under any circumstances it is still true that what was characteristic of the Reformation was not a setting aside of tradition but an attempt to distinguish between "true" and "false" tradition, and to maintain Scripture as the decisive factor in making the distinction. In other words, Scripture was the superior authority by which the validity of all "tradition" must be established.

It is beyond the scope of this work to provide an adequate analysis of how the Reformation in practice sought to apply its fundamental view of the relationship between Scripture and tradition, nor can we follow the various ramifications of this problem in post-Reformation history. A few questions related to this problem will indeed be discussed in the following sections. Our chief interest, however, is directed toward modern problems, especially those connected with the ecumenical movement.

In the preceding we spoke about "tradition" without defining the meaning of this word. Now we must define its meaning more accurately and suggest the chief points of view from which we are to look at the concept in the following discussion. The word has been understood in various ways in the course of time. When tradition was spoken of as distinct from Scripture during the first centuries of the church, it referred mostly to a few circulating reports and notices about Christ, the apostles, and the early church, such as were supplied for instance in Eusebius' *Church History*. None of the church fathers regarded this tradition as in any sense equal to Scripture or to any great extent trustworthy. To Irenaeus the tradition was nothing else than the apostolic tradition as this was recorded in Scripture. Later on the concept of tradition came to refer to the teaching of the church, especially to the confessional formulas which had been authoritatively defined by the church. The Reformation documents generally speak of *traditions, traditiones humanae*, as referring to all kinds of ecclesiastical prescriptions which regulated the life in the church in various ways, practices of worship, duties Christians were supposed to observe, and so on. The Council of Trent maintained that alongside of the written tradition there was also an oral tradition which the church administered and to which it could refer as occasion demanded. The Roman theologians to whom we have listened in the preceding sections want to substitute another conception of the tradition in which the reference to certain "realities" given to the church is the essential. We could multiply examples of these conceptions of the meaning of the tradition. What we have presented is sufficient to show that we are dealing with a concept which has varied greatly in the course of time and is, therefore, rather vague.

Church and tradition belong inseparably together. In its widest sense the concept of tradition refers to that which in course of time has grown up in the church. Naturally not all of this can be designated as "tradition." Much of it has had only a transitory character. We can speak of tradition only in regard to factors which have left permanent marks, and which have to a greater or lesser degree marked the life of the church or of the various denominations, factors that are met with everywhere, in the whole history of the church and in all the various communions. There has never been, nor will there ever be, a communion independent of the traditional elements connected with the history of the church. No communion has ever been merely a copy or a reproduction of the biblical *ecclesia*. To be sure, programs of that kind have been proposed, which were intended to establish a purely "biblical congregational order" or a purely biblical order of service. But these programs have never succeeded. The idea that a church could embody a biblical reproduction with the elimination of everything connected with tradition is an illusion. In one way or another they are always dependent on earlier tradition; and in one way or another they also create their own tradition.

When we look at the numerous denominations in Christendom, we note at once that each one has its own character and special tradition. There are therefore a multiplicity of *traditions*. In this case the plural form is appropriate. This by no means implies that the various denominations as such would be characterized by a stereotyped uniformity, nor that the different traditions are separated from one another by immovable walls. The real situation is that great differences may be found within one and the same communion, and that contact across confessional boundaries may have the result that one tradition more or less influences another. It may lead and sometimes has led to a weakening of and uncertainty in regard to one's own tradition.

If we look at what is happening in the ecumenical sphere, there appears another aspect of the matter. Here earlier isolation has broken down, new connections have been established, and older, rigid, controversial problems have been revised. But at the same time we find a growing appreciation of what is found to be essential and indispensable in one's own tradition. We may indeed speak of a tension between these tendencies, but it would nevertheless be wrong to speak of them as antagonistic to one another.

The many denominations have come from the same root. Behind the individual traditions stands the common tradition from the time of the "undivided" church. Appreciation of this common tradition by the various communions has varied to a great extent. The reason appreciation at present may be said to be growing, even in areas where it had been relatively weak, is not only that those engaged in ecumenical endeavors must necessarily be concerned with the common history of Christianity. Involved also is the fact that our present research has emphasized the connection between the ancient church and early Christianity much more than was true of exegetical and dogmatic research in the past.

A marginal note may be added here. We have just noted that Irenaeus identified the New Testament with the apostolic tradition. In the same way it has often been said in modern times that the New Testament is a compendium of the original, apostolic *tradition*. No real objection can be made against the statement. It is in evident agreement with the facts. But if from one point of view the New Testament may be seen under the aspect of tradition, this in no sense means a downgrading of the authority of Scripture, or an elimination of the problem of the relationship between Scripture and tradition. Precisely as a primary, apostolic tradition the New Testament contains the fundamental and for-all-time decisive message of God's act in Christ. Whether or not we call the New Testament writings primary apostolic tradition is mostly a matter of terminology. That it *can* be so designated does not jeopardize at all the primacy of Scripture in relation to all other tradition in the church.

Church and tradition are therefore inseparably connected.

133

Tradition is involved in all phases of the church's life. If we are to be clear on the meaning of this tradition, we cannot speak about it simply in generalities. It will be necessary to define the chief points under which the rich and variegated tradition material can be arranged. There are especially three chief contexts to be considered: doctrine, worship, order—*doctrina, liturgia, ordo.* Looking at the modern ecumenical discussion, we find that it revolves around these three factors. It is obvious that questions about doctrine must play a large role when different communions confront one another. From the very beginning of the ecumenical movement interest in the question of order has been exceedingly great. The problem of worship has not from the beginning been of such great moment. It has, however, been given more and more attention. It was not an accident that one of the two volumes that served as a preparation for the Conference in Lund (1952) was entitled *Ways of Worship.* This pointed up the fact that *liturgia,* in this word's widest sense, is one of the chief factors in the tradition. It need hardly be said that these areas stand in intimate relationship with one another. This will be illustrated in the following presentation. What happens in one area has obvious repercussions in the others.

If we review the statements that have been made so far about the relationship between Scripture and tradition, we may establish that all of them have wanted in some way to maintain the primacy of Scripture. This is also true of the Roman contribution. In the tradition, says Congar, "the Holy Scripture is the normative rule." It may be further stated that all denominations are dependent on tradition. There is no communion in which church life, as it appears in doctrine, worship, and order, is in any sense a mere reproduction of the proclamation and directives of the Bible. We might construct a theory that church life ought to be nothing else than a reproduction, but no such theory can be consistently put into practice. That it cannot succeed is due to the fact that the Bible does not contain a unified and fixed doctrine, a unified and fixed worship, or a unified and fixed church order. Since none the less everyone in Christianity in one way or another defends the primacy of Scripture over against tradition, it becomes of utmost importance to explicate in what this "primacy" really consists. From this point of view we will analyze the three chief areas of the tradition in the next three sections. Before we do so, however, we will say a few words about how the primacy of Scripture is not to be understood.

In the first place it must not be understood in a formal-legalistic sense. This would in reality mean a negative attitude toward the tradition which has grown up in the church. Scripture and tradition would then be regarded as competing in principle with one another. Nothing could be accepted which was not expressly established in Scripture, and every injunction would be equally obligating. This would mean that the fundamental conception of Scripture would be something else than that of Scripture itself. Instead of being a message about God's redemptive and church-creating act in Christ it would be transformed into a law.

The relationship of Scripture to tradition cannot be expressed under the aspect of evolution. Just as it is obvious that tradition interpreted and expressed what was latent in the biblical message and thus so to speak exploited the riches of Scripture, so it is obvious that not everything that has been offered in tradition stands in agreement with the biblical content. Tradition as a whole cannot simply be likened to a great tree grown from the seed of the gospel, as Cardinal Newman suggested; nor can it be validated by Schleiermacher's phrase, "Ever more perfectly the Holy Spirit permeates the whole." While legalism takes a negative attitude toward tradition within the church, the evolutionary perspective manifests its inability to distinguish between true and false tradition. The former standpoint results in fact in a denial of the activity of the Spirit in the church. The latter, on the other hand, confuses the Spirit with what happens in the church. The Spirit becomes, in Schleiermacher's words, *Gemeingeist*. The first fails to take into account what is said in John 16:13: "When the Spirit of truth comes, he will guide you into all the truth;" the second ignores what is said in the following verse: "He will take what is mine and declare it to you."

14. *DOCTRINA*

The question about *doctrina* will be discussed here as a part of the question about the relationship between Scripture and tradition. It means that our attention must be focused on how the primacy of Scripture appears in reference to that part of tradition which constitutes *doctrina*.

If at the start we should ask what place "doctrine" has in Lutheran communions, we will easily discover that there are two opposite conceptions. Many would no doubt question whether there really is a solid and reliable "teaching" in a Lutheran church such as the Swedish church. They would point out that different ecclesiastical tendencies struggle with one another and sometimes exist side by side without any mutual recognition. They would especially call attention to theological conflicts and antitheses which may sometimes concern essential matters. On the basis of such factors they might draw the conclusion that the teaching is not very firmly fixed, and that what we see here is a church on the way to dissolution.

If, on the contrary, we take note of what has appeared in ecumenical discussion, we would discover an entirely different picture. Many representatives of other communions would without question assert that "Lutherans" take a conspicuously strict attitude toward "doctrine." Some few would even go still further and describe the Lutheran churches as doctrinaire, that they are indulgent and even passive in regard to questions of worship and order, but just about unreasonable in matters of doctrine. They could also point to the exceedingly reserved attitude the Lutherans have shown in regard to church unions. To be sure, there have been cases where a Lutheran church has taken part in some union discussions with non-Lutheran communions, but the results have hitherto been negative—on account of "doctrine."

As we begin the discussion of the relationship between Scripture and *doctrina,* we must first define what we mean by *doctrina*. If we examine the common usage, we find that the word "doctrine" may be used in two distinct senses: on the one hand, as more or less equivalent to confession, and, on the other hand, as a designation of the continuous theological presentations of the content of the Christian faith. When we speak of "the doctrine of a certain church," we mean primarily the fixed confession of this church. In comparison theological presentations appear as a secondary element within the "tradition" of the respective churches. None of these presentations can claim to represent what these churches "teach" and confess. Since in the previous sections we have already fully discussed the confession of the Reformation and its relationship to the biblical confession and to that of the ancient church, we may confine our discussion of this part of the matter to a few reflections and then examine the theological aspect of the subject in more detail.

There has been, as we know, a great deal of discussion of what we mean by a confessional church. Without entering upon a discussion of this subject we may affirm at once that a Lutheran church is a confessional church. It points to definitely formulated confessions, partly from the ancient church, and partly from the time of the Reformation. At the same time the Reformation confessions have declared with utter clarity that the Bible is the chief authority. They themselves would not claim to be anything more than a testimony and a directing guide to that which is given in the Bible. This means that the relationship between the Bible and the confessions is twofold. The confession is an apology. The purpose of the confessions is to be a defense against misinterpretations of the biblical message. At the same time the confession places itself under the control of the Bible and is subject to continual testing by the biblical word. This means that the Reformation confession does not claim that its formulations are to be regarded as final and definitive. We have seen previously one of the Orthodox theologians claim that the decisions of the old councils are to be interpreted "historically and spiritually." This conforms to what the Reformation confessions state about their own character: they must be interpreted historically and spiritually—in the light of the Bible.

That the church is a confessional church appears not only in the fact that it possesses a number of confessions from ancient times. It makes itself known also in the confession the church continually makes in its worship and its holy rites. It cannot really be sufficiently emphasized that the confession of the church lives in its liturgy. This point has too often been ignored. The liturgy makes the confession come alive. It does so not only because the two classic Christian confessions of faith are a part of the worship service, and thus have an obvious and constitutive

137

significance for the life of the church. This is in itself a very important point. But this is just a part of the life-giving work which the liturgy performs. The liturgy itself as a whole is permeated by the threefold confession: that of the Bible, of the ancient church, and of the Reformation. The stability of the liturgy preserves the continuity of the confession. At the same time the changes which may be made from time to time, and which are legitimate insofar as they make the biblical message clearer, richer, and more accessible, indicate that the confession is a *living* reality, not a stereotyped repetition.

In comparison with this confession of the church which appears in various documents, the *doctrina* which appears in theological presentations is a secondary and much more changeable element. The theological task cannot be confined to a reproduction of the content of the confessions, especially since the confessions recognize themselves as subject to the control of the Bible. A theology can be "confessional" only insofar as the confessional element—its own "tradition" in the sphere of doctrine—serves to explicate the meaning of the biblical message. From this point of view the theological task is always an interpretation of the Bible. But no matter how essential the exegetical work is for the purely historical explication of the character and content of the biblical writings, theology cannot be satisfied with being merely exegesis. Theology must also relate the biblical message to contemporary life. It must seek to present it in such a way that it becomes accessible and relevant to the given situation. Each age presents its own peculiar demands. So does our own time, which is largely characterized by strangeness to the Bible, not only to what usually is referred to as the biblical world view but also to its central religious content.

If the theological task then is to make the biblical message clear and relevant in the contemporary situation, it is threatened by two dangers to which its history plainly bears witness. The one is for theology to be satisfied with a mere reproduction of the biblical thought world. This means that we look upon the Bible as a uniform textbook in dogmatics. In that way the real character of the Bible is denied. The Bible is not a uniform body of dogma. It presents a homogeneous message, but from a doctrinal point of view this message meets us in manifold variations. Consequently faithfulness to the message is not the same as a slavish adherence to the letter which identifies religious content with external appearance. This slavery to the letter lacks that firm grip on the central message of the Bible which is fundamental and necessary if the biblical content is to be expressed in all its fulness, and if its religious message is to come alive in a milieu which is completely different from that of two thousand years ago.

The other danger is for biblical content to become accommodated to what is regarded as the contemporary "world view." Biblical content is weighed and appraised, accepted or rejected on the basis of a foreign criterion. Post-Reformation theology furnishes many examples of this kind of treatment, from the rationalizations of the Enlightenment to modern attempts at demythologizing. The purpose of such attempts as the latter may be highly commendable. The desire to make the content come alive is evident. Theology should certainly not be satisfied with sanctioning any and all ways of expressing the content. It knows that the essential is not the garb but the content hidden behind it. But accommodations, of whatever kind they may be, nevertheless lead theology astray because here, as in the other case, it has lost the firm grip on the central message of the Bible.

We must emphasize two facts in this connection. First, the "stumbling block" of the Christian message is in reality the same in all ages. Second, the fundamental conditions of human life are likewise the same from generation to generation. The theology of accommodation is intended to eliminate "stumbling blocks," especially those connected with the changed world view. Even such problems may indeed need to be examined by theology. But the real stumbling block is not at this point. It can appear so only to one for whom the garb is more important than the religious content. The real "stumbling block" lies precisely in the central message. This was the same for the ancient people, for "Jews and Greeks," as it is for the people of the space age. *This* stumbling block neither can nor should be eliminated. It consists in the fact that God's decisive act of redemption is localized and concentrated in a human figure at the mid-point of history; or, to express it in the Bible's own words, in the fact that in Jesus Christ "the whole fulness of deity dwells bodily" (Col. 2:9). Furthermore, whatever profound changes in the conditions of human life may have taken place, the fundamental condition of human life nevertheless remains the same down through the ages, because life is lived now as formerly under the conditions of sin and death. The message which brings the promise of redemption from sin and death, therefore, will always be relevant to human life.

When we spoke above of the "dangers" which confront the interpretation of Scripture, we touched also on the problem of critical and historical research into the Bible. During recent centuries hardly any other problem has claimed the attention of theology to so great an extent. This is true especially in the case of Protestant theology. That this should be so is quite natural. Historical-critical research began here, and here it could develop freely without hindrance. Here also the view of the Bible which made the authority of Scripture dependent on a theory of inspiration claiming divine inspiration for every letter of the Bible had been most consistently expounded. The contrast was overwhelming. On the one hand was a theory of the Bible which completely eliminated the human element, and on the other hand a research which not only irrefutably demonstrated this human element, but also was in principle intent on investigating the Bible precisely as a human historical document. Under these conditions it is not strange that this historical-critical investigation was on the verge of undermining and dissolving the authority of the Bible. Nor is it strange that on this account there should arise conflicts between the church and theology, because to the church the Bible is never merely a human historical document. It is first and last the Word of God.

The problem posed by historical-critical research, however, is not at all an exclusive problem of the Protestant churches. It is of universal proportions. We have found it also among those Roman theologians to whom we have listened. Indeed, their argumentation claims that the Roman church is more capable than "Protestant" theology of asserting and safeguarding the authority of Scripture. Their recurrent fundamental point of view is that

the interpretation of Scripture in Protestantism is completely in
the hands of the "doctors," or, in other words, of theology and
its shifting opinions; while, on the contrary, the *magisterium*
of the Roman church furnishes a secure guarantee of the integrity
of biblical interpretation. They do not by any means want to
dismiss the historical investigation of the Bible. They speak
rather, as has been done in several recent papal encyclicals, of
both the necessity and the value of research. But at the same
time the *magisterium* of the church, incorporated in the Pope,
and on the basis of the authority it possesses, exercises a necessary and regulatory control. According to Congar, this does not
mean that the *magisterium* sets itself up as the judge of Scripture, but it means that through its testimony the *magisterium*
watches over the interpretation of Scripture. When the Reformation rejected the authority of the *magisterium,* he says, the
church was delivered over to the *"magisterium* of the doctors,"
i.e., to the shifting interpretations of theological research. Divo
Barsotti speaks in a similar way. "It is not through the interpretation of Scripture by the doctors, as in the case of the
Protestants, but through the testimony of the bishops that the
church speaks and God reveals himself as present and active in
the midst of humanity." [6] The identification of Christ and the
church is "the fundamental basis of the *magisterium's* infallibility
in the church." Infallibility may also be established by reference
to the Spirit. "It is the union of the Spirit and the church which
is the fundamental basis of the actions of the hierarchy and especially of the effectiveness and infallibility of the *magisterium*." [7]

When we listen to statements of this kind, it would seem
that concern for the authority of Scripture undeniably has its
most secure stronghold in the Roman church, and that Rome
provides a sure guarantee of the integrity of Scripture, while on
the contrary the Protestant churches surrender the scriptural
Word to shifting theological interpretations and opinions. Is this
criticism of the "Protestant" position valid? And further, is it
true that the authority of the word of the Bible is more securely
safeguarded in Rome? The very fact that such questions may

[6] Barsotti, *op. cit.,* pp. 180-81.
[7] *Ibid.,* 186.

be seriously asked indicates the impossibility of being satisfied with clichés, according to which the Protestant position would pit the Scriptures against the church, and the Roman vice versa; as if Rome were not concerned about Scripture, and as if, according to the evangelical point of view, the problem of the authority of Scripture could be solved without taking the church into account at all. These problems are too fundamental and complicated for such an easy and nonchalant solution.

Rome tries to solve these difficulties by exercising censorship over theological studies. In order to get permission to print and distribute theological books they must obtain official imprimatur. The evangelical church does not exercise any such censorship. There is an unlimited freedom of research. This fact indicates a very high regard for theological research. But this does not mean that the "doctors" have been elevated to the position of the highest court, or that they have been given some kind of infallibility. The essential position of the evangelical church is characterized by two factors. It depends first on the insight that all research is relative, and second—and especially—on the conviction that the gospel the church has to proclaim is one and unchangeable. The relativity of research is demonstrated in its history, which manifests many mistakes but also indicates how it continually corrects itself. It cannot be denied that historical criticism has created many problems for the church. At the same time it has given the church invaluable and profound knowledge of the context of human history in which the history of God's dealings with humanity lies imbedded. But no matter how profound the historical insights it may provide, it can never as historical research either controvert or verify the Bible as the Word of God. To arrive at such decisions is beyond the capabilities of historical criticism. As soon as we consider God's revelation and his work, we have moved from the area of research to that of faith.

What takes place in the church, Christ's continuing redemptive activity, expands our vision. Through the activity of the Spirit the biblical message is revealed as divine. The stability and unchangeableness of the message depends on the fact that Christ is "the same yesterday and today and for ever" (Heb.

13:8). As the risen and living Lord he continues here and now the work of reconciliation he accomplished once and for all on the cross. What "guarantees" the stability and integrity of this message is neither historical criticism of the Bible nor any ecclesiastical authorities, but only the Holy Spirit who functions in the church. "No one can say 'Jesus is Lord' except by the Holy Spirit" (I Cor. 12:3). It is the Spirit who "will guide you into all the truth." He keeps "the truth" alive in the church of Christ by glorifying Christ. "He will take what is mine and declare it to you" (John 16:13-14).

But the guidance of the Spirit does not mean that no errors or obscuring of the truth can arise in the church. No communion has any guarantee that it will not happen, neither the evangelical churches nor the church of Rome. "The truth" is always subject to suppression. The promise of the guidance of the Spirit means that in spite of everything truth will be preserved. There is no other guarantee of its preservation than the fact that the function of the Spirit in the church never ceases.

In and by itself it is quite understandable for Rome to make the claim that the development which started with the Reformation resulted in having the interpretation of Scripture handed over to the shifting opinions of "the doctors." It would be unrealistic to claim that this observation was entirely without justification. If we look at the relationship between the Protestant churches and historical criticism of the Bible, we will find *both* a negative and unsympathetic attitude on the part of the *magisterium* of the church *and* a tendency to follow uncritically the gyrations of theological research—on the one hand an entrenchment behind untenable theories of inspiration, and on the other hand a willingness to accept at face value the various interpretations of the Bible which have quickly succeeded one another. The research of the two last centuries has provided us with invaluable and enriching knowledge, but it has also placed the churches and their preaching before difficult problems. The principal reason for this has not been historical investigation as such, but the fact that the interpretation of the Bible has often been made on the basis of historical ideas and presuppositions which are foreign to the Bible itself and have therefore resulted in interpretations contrary to the nature of the Bible. There is good reason for saying, however, that research, as it constantly corrects itself, has seen more and more clearly the illegitimacy of judging the Bible by criteria foreign to its nature, and that as a result it has been able to give a clearer exposition of the uniqueness of the Bible and of the continuity and unity found in the midst of multiplicity.

In reference to the integrity of the Christian message, Roman theologians as well as evangelical refer to the guidance of the Spirit. But the difference is that while evangelical theologians think of the function of the Spirit in conjunction with the scriptural Word of God, the Roman theologians localize the Spirit in the *magisterium* of the church. In and by itself there can be no objection to the fact that those who have been given the office to serve the church in the Word and the sacraments have thereby also been given a special responsibility to watch over and preserve the purity of the gospel. But it becomes a different matter when the Spirit is localized in the *magisterium* of the church and its members are clothed with infallibility. The guidance of the Spirit becomes identified with the guidance of the infallible occupants of churchly office. The responsibility is thereby changed into a power that in fact is unlimited. The purpose of this identification of the Spirit and the *magisterium* is obviously to create security. By virtue of its alleged infallibility the *magisterium* of the church controls the interpretation of the Bible. It fixes the limits within which interpretation is permitted to move. Furthermore, the *magisterium,* as concentrated in the authority of the Pope and with the claim of infallibility, makes all decisions regarding the doctrine of the church.

The question is, how much guarantee and security are really achieved. As we have seen, modern Roman theologians do not want to talk about Scripture and tradition as two equal authorities. They prefer to characterize Scripture and tradition as a unity within which, as Congar says, Scripture is the fundamental element. This attitude is connected with a stronger emphasis on Scripture within the modern Roman church. But though we may speak here unequivocally about a Bible renaissance, it is equally obvious that there are other tendencies which lead away from Scripture to a freedom from its authority. These later tendencies are connected with and in reality flow automatically from the theory of the infallibility of the *magisterium* in all matters of doctrine. The two Marian dogmas promulgated by the Pope in 1854 and 1950 are incontestable witnesses to this fact. In neither case have they shown any concern to justify these dogmas on the basis of Scripture or even the tradition of the ancient church. In reality these two dogmas are foreign to Scripture and contrary to the ancient tradition of the church. They have been based on "the living consciousness of faith" in the modern church. In other words, when the infallible doctrinal office established the dogmas, it was sanctioning what had grown up in folk piety. It is characteristic that, after the latest Marian dogma was established, Pius XII declared that it was the duty of theology "to show how a teaching defined by the church is contained in the revealed sources in just that meaning which has been defined by the church." [8] This means, as is clearly stated, that Scripture and the older tradition of the church are to be interpreted on the basis of what the official teaching of the church is today. This indicates with perfect clarity that the infallible office of teaching by no means guarantees the integrity of the interpretation of Scripture. On the contrary, it results in a dissolution of integrity. The ecclesiastical teaching office goes its own way and tries to compel intractable Scripture to follow.

15. *LITURGIA*

As we have already pointed out, liturgical questions have aroused a growing interest within the modern ecumenical movement. While the discussions at first were concentrated on *doctrina* and *ordo,* the problems of the worship service have gradually become a third central concern. Without doubt the reason for this is that in general these problems have been given more attention in all of Christendom, and that, even where they have traditionally been regarded as secondary, their essential importance for the life of the church has been recognized. If we were to write a book on the liturgical renewal during recent decades,

[8] P. E. Persson, "Vad är romerskt?" in *Svensk teologisk kvartalskrift,* 1958, p. 26.

we would have at our disposal an extensive mass of material from different communions, even from those within which liturgy previously had been given scant attention.

There are also, however, immediate reasons why ecumenical discussions have gone in this direction. A fundamental presupposition for ecumenical endeavors is obviously that the various communions learn to know one another. We have good reasons for saying that worship life is well equipped to provide inside information. It reveals the character of the various communions. We learn to know them from within. But this is not all. Worship life has a twofold relationship to Christian unity. On the one hand, it is a strong incentive to unity across boundaries. The common devotional services which are a regular part of ecumenical meetings have more than anything else revealed an inner fellowship which no confessional boundaries are able to destroy. On the other hand, worship life manifests the deep schism. Nothing can emphasize more forcefully or more accusingly manifest this schism than the fact that fellowship is broken off at the Table of the Lord. It is not surprising that liturgy has become a chief subject of discussion in ecumenical meetings.

We use the word *liturgia* here in its widest significance. It designates the whole worship life of the church with the inclusion of preaching, celebration of the Lord's Supper, prayer, confession, and praise. Our main question is: what significance does the primacy of the Bible have for the worship life of the church? The New Testament bears clear witness to the fact that worship was the center of life in the ancient church. Later research has enriched our knowledge of this subject. It has shown that biblical writings contain far more references to worship life than was earlier suspected. But no matter how much, by glimpses, we learn of worship in the ancient church and of its constituent parts, we seek in vain for a rigidly clear-cut order of service which might serve as a norm for all time to come. Sometimes in the latter days of the church the demand has been made that the worship service should be patterned according to the New Testament order, but this is a demand that cannot be met. Worship life has taken various forms within the different denominations, but no worship service of any communion has ever been or ever could be a copy of that of the ancient church. The normativeness of Scripture, in other words, is not that of a fixed ritual. It does not mean that an order of service valid for all time has been fixed. The directive Scripture provides concerns the content and character of the liturgy.

It is not our purpose to present a detailed analysis of worship life in the ancient church and thus on that basis seek to explain what the biblical norm means for the liturgy. We have to limit ourselves to a few reflections on the basis of those liturgical perspectives which have already been touched upon. It will be profitable to pay particular attention to Bouyer's criticism of the liturgical development both in his own church and in the Reformation.

Bouyer's book was written to serve the interests of liturgical renewal within the Roman church. The liturgical decline against which he contends had its roots in the Middle Ages. Pious practices which appeared then cannot by any means be regarded as exemplary; they are rather a departure from the spirit of true liturgy. Bouyer remarks in this connection that "the Oxford Movement" in the Church of England of a hundred years ago borrowed from Rome just such things as are now regarded by contemporary Roman authorities as liturgical weaknesses. One example is the enthusiasm for the Benediction of the Blessed Sacrament. Neither the baroque period nor Romanticism succeeded in producing a liturgical renewal. The efforts toward renewal which have appeared lately have very properly returned to the church fathers. Here we find in reality the key to what is of permanent value in the tradition of the church. This, says Bouyer, is really self-evident "since the Patristic was certainly the most creative of all periods in this field." [9] This reference to the church fathers does not mean, however, that Bouyer would isolate them from the tradition of the church as a whole. Renewal cannot be obtained by copying the fathers, but by finding guidance in their "living ideas."

His reference to the fathers is co-ordinated with a reference to the Bible. Liturgical renewal, as described by Bouyer, must be

[9] Bouyer, *Piety,* p. 21.

L   147

inseparably connected with "the Bible renaissance." The liturgy as a whole, he says, may be described both as "the Word of God" and as "God's action." The liturgy is the place where God's word of the New Covenant is proclaimed; it is also therefore the place of the new creation.[10] The mystery of the Sacrament and the biblical Word mutually interact with one another. It is fruitless to "return" the liturgy to men without at the same time giving them full and immediate access to the Bible. The Bible becomes illuminated by the reality of the sacramental *mystery;* at the same time the Bible leads us to "a full liturgical life," when it becomes "the supernatural world of all our thoughts and meditation and the food of our prayers." [11]

In these statements about the Sacrament and the Bible we find the principal word in Bouyer's book: *the mystery.* What does this word mean? The background of Bouyer's definition of the mystery we find in his criticism of the "extra-liturgical" practices of piety. He constantly characterizes these practices as having lost the risen and living Christ. The presence of Christ, which is the object of adoration, is conceived of as "a common, human presence," "a substitute for the Lord's visible presence during his life on earth." The danger of such devotional practices, according to Bouyer, is not only that they obscure the central worship service, the Mass itself, but also that they obscure the meaning of the mystery in the Mass. The thought of the presence of Christ in the mystery is in danger of being eliminated. The result is "the most crude expression of a mistaken view of the Eucharistic presence, as though it were the localized and natural presence of a being who can still suffer and die; and of a no less mistaken view of the Cross, as being a human defeat and not the divine victory." [12] It ends in "a mysticism very far from that of the New Testament and the fathers." [13] On the basis of such starting points the idea arose that "the Mass was meant to reproduce the Passion by a kind of mimetic reproduction, as if its purpose were "to suggest not

[10] *Ibid.,* p. 30.
[11] *Ibid.,* p. 254.
[12] *Ibid.,* p. 252.
[13] *Ibid.,* p. 248.

only the physical, but also a carnal presence of our Lord." [14]

The criticism to which we have listened indicates the direction of Bouyer's thought in regard to "the mystery." The Lord's Supper may be studied from various points of view. In his synopsis of the various aspects of the Lord's Supper Bouyer starts from the exposition of the various aspects of the Lord's Supper which Yngve Brilioth has presented in his book, *Eucharistic Faith and Practice*. In agreement with Brilioth Bouyer speaks of the Lord's Supper as communion, sacrifice, thanksgiving, remembrance—and mystery. Bouyer emphasizes that the mystery includes and permeates all the other aspects. This is the center around which everything moves, and it is therefore also the theme to which Bouyer constantly returns.

The world into which the liturgy introduces us is "the meeting-point of the world of the resurrection with this very world of ours in which we must live, suffer and die." [15] This statement from one of the last pages of the book may be said to suggest a fundamental motif in Bouyer's interpretation of the meaning of the mystery. In the beginning of the book Bouyer makes the following thematic statement: the mystery is "the re-enactment in, by and for the Church of the Act of our Lord which accomplishes our salvation, that is, His Passion and Death in the fulness of their final effects,—the Resurrection, the communication of saving grace to mankind and the final consummation of all things." The decisive element is the continual renewal of and participation in the redemptive work of Christ in the church. This conception of the liturgy, he says, "is entirely different from that of imaginative or theatrical representation or from any physically realistic repetition." It is the clue to a right understanding of the liturgy, the clue which began to fade during the Middle Ages. "And it is this clue which the Baroque period had lost so completely that it kept in view only a shell of the liturgy— a shell which was so much the more externally adorned and built over as the reality inside tended to be forgotten." [16]

We understand very well why Bouyer's criticism is directed

[14] *Ibid.*, p. 16.
[15] *Ibid.*, p. 267.
[16] *Ibid.*, p. 18.

toward devotional practices which fail to include the risen and living Lord. In a summarizing exposition of the meaning of the mystery[17] he places the emphasis on that redemptive act which takes place in the liturgy. With a reference to the words of Paul in I Corinthians 10:16 Bouyer describes the eucharistic celebration of the ancient church in these words: The disciples "knew that the risen Lord was again with them, that in His apostles He was now again re-enacting what he had done once for all, that in Him, through them, the almighty and all-creative Word of God was nourishing with the true bread of heaven the new 'Qahal,' the new family of God, and so making one body of all those who had now eaten the *one bread."* The *mysterium* of the liturgy is the continuing redemptive activity. Bouyer says, therefore, as he summarizes his analysis of the mystery, that the mystery is finally God himself, the divine *agape,* the creative and redemptive love which is a pure gift. The mystery means that God's plan for humanity is realized through Christ, God's all-creative Word. Bouyer, like Barsotti, emphasizes heavily the importance of the inseparable unity of "the Word" and the Sacrament. The Word is present in the Sacrament as something essential. "The liturgy makes us hear God's Word in Christ, and it makes us experience in our own lives the power of that Word of God as it is shown forth in the cross." In this Word God gives himself, for "His Word is nothing else than that love which is His divine life and absolute self-giving." [18]

We must now discuss the historical and ideological context of these liturgical ideas. Bouyer himself has indicated how this context is to be understood. The liturgical renewal stems from the church fathers and the Bible. But it is not a question of mechanically reproducing the liturgy of the ancient church, while ignoring intervening history, but rather of gaining inspiration from "the living ideas" of the church fathers. However, no liturgical renewal is possible except in connection with the renaissance of the Bible. The Bible is "the framework and ever-living source of all authentic Christianity." [19] There is no ques-

[17] *Ibid.,* pp. 126-27.
[18] *Ibid.,* p. 106.
[19] *Ibid.,* p. 253.

tion but that Roman efforts toward liturgical renewal, which Bouyer represents, have gathered their inspiration and strength from this source. His many sharply critical statements bear witness to this fact. The same is true of his direct tie with the liturgy of the ancient church. One indication of this is that Bouyer, as he refers to the richly developed prefaces of the ancient church, emphasizes the central place of the Preface in the Mass. The principal witness to the connection with the ancient church—and the Bible—we find, however, in the interpretation of the mystery that we have just reviewed. The presupposition of this interpretation is the synoptic view of the cross and the resurrection which characterized the biblical and the ancient church's conception, but which later was to a greater or lesser degree lost during the Middle Ages. When the liturgy is determined by this synoptic view, its true spirit is preserved. Then the liturgy becomes a continuous redemptive act. "Everything that is 'announced' to us in the liturgy is announced, not only as a part of the past, but as the one great reality of the present also, as well as of the future." [20] In other words, the liturgy is *a means of grace* through which the members of the church are made partakers of the grace which finally is nothing less than God's *agape* in Christ.

The historical and ideological context of his conception is further illumined by his statement concerning the sacrifice and the presence of Christ in the Sacrament. In both cases his statements have a critical tone. Bouyer opposes the idea that the Mass, "as we often hear it proclaimed," means that our sacrifice is united with that of Christ himself. "In Christianity there is not and cannot be any sacrifice other than Christ's own sacrifice: no idea could be more opposed to the true spirit of the liturgy than the supposition that we could bring to the altar some sacrifice of our own, complete in itself, which we ourselves have made prior to our meeting Christ at the altar, and then add it to His own Cross. Nothing can be added to the Cross: we are only to leave our lives and ourselves in the hands of Christ so as to be taken into His Cross." [21]

[20] *Ibid.,* p. 80.
[21] *Ibid.,* p. 169.

We find in Bouyer emphatic expressions of Christ's *active* presence in the liturgy. The mystery means that "the life-giving reality of His Cross is given to us by the risen Lord." "The actuality of the Mystery is simply the actuality of the risen Christ. As He stands in the glory of His resurrection, like the Lamb slain but glorious, He has found the way to hold for us and to communicate to us all the healing power and life-giving reality of His Cross." [22] In further elaborating on the nature of this presence, Bouyer tells us that "in some forms of modern Catholicism" there is "an overemphasis on the real presence," which has not only forced aside some important aspects of the Sacrament—communion, sacrifice, thanksgiving, remembrance—but in addition has rather "degraded than exalted the mystery itself." Such an overemphasis on the Real Presence may be avoided provided attention is not one-sidedly directed toward the sacramental bread and wine but in addition toward "two other realities." "If there is a necessity, first of all, to consider the presence of Christ as victim in the eucharistic elements, we must not for that reason neglect His presence as high priest in the whole hierarchy. Christ will be present in the elements only because He is present in the man who is to preside over the *synaxis* and to say the thanksgiving in Christ's own name, this presence being brought about through the apostolic succession. And, thirdly, Christ is to be present in the whole body of the Church, for the Church enjoys the eucharistic presence only to be made one, *in* Christ and *with* Christ." [23] To this exposition of the Real Presence we want to add two marginal remarks. In the first place, Bouyer's criticism of the overemphasis on the Real Presence does not in reality concern the Real Presence as such, but rather one-sided attention to the elements of the Lord's Supper. In the second place, in this argumentation the primary presence of Christ is connected with the hierarchy and conditioned upon the apostolic succession.

It is natural that Bouyer should be just as anxious to dissociate himself from the Reformation as he is to emphasize his kinship with the ancient church. We have already touched on his criticism

[22] *Ibid.*, p. 184.
[23] *Ibid.*, pp. 80-81.

of the Reformation. In taking up this theme again, we want to determine what is fiction and what is fact in Bouyer's criticism, and especially illuminate the historical and ideological context of the Reformation.

A frequently recurring point of view in Bouyer is that the Reformation was dependent on the decadent developments of the Middle Ages. His statements on this point are conspicuously unmodulated. Among other things he claims that the Reformation ignored "the mystery," that in line with the later Middle Ages it held one-sidedly to the passion motif with the elimination of the resurrection, and that it therefore was characterized by the sentimental pity for the suffering Christ characteristic of the piety of the later Middle Ages. As we have already indicated, this is a complete reversal of the true facts. To be sure it is self-evident that the Reformation does not stand isolated, and that it stands in both a negative and a positive relationship to the Middle Ages. Thus, for example, the part that the sacrament of penance played during the Middle Ages undeniably presented questions of vital importance for the Reformation. But the Reformation was not dependent on the Middle Ages in the sense that Bouyer means. On the contrary, there is unquestionably a much closer connection between the Reformation and Bouyer's own criticism than he is willing to admit. His criticism of typically Medieval practices of piety, of a one-sidedly physical interpretation of the presence of Christ in the Sacrament, and especially his positive interpretation of the meaning of "the mystery," is made for the purpose of permitting "the liturgy" to appear as "a means of grace" through which the church and its members become partakers of God's *agape* in Christ. Such a purpose is in any case akin to the Reformation, because there was nothing dearer to its heart than this—that the liturgy, in the widest sense of the word, should serve as *a means of grace*.

It has been correctly pointed out that Luther's idea of "the Word" as a means of grace represented something new in relation to the Middle Ages. It is well known that in this respect the Reformation thought primarily of the spoken Word or preaching. The new element did not consist in a demand that there should be more preaching than formerly. It was not a question of quantity but of quality. The true meaning and purpose of the sermon is to function as "a means of grace," as an instrument through which the Spirit continually makes Christ and with him also God's redemptive mercy, his *agape*, effectively present. It is obvious that on the basis of this new conception of the purpose of the sermon it would later receive a more prominent place in worship life than it had previously had. The same is true also in regard to the Sacrament. The polemic against Rome did not by any means intend to set aside the Sacrament. The point was not that Rome had overemphasized the Sacrament, but on the contrary that its character as a means of grace had been obscured and neglected. This is the very heart of the criticism the Reformation directed against contemporary practices of the sacrifice of the Mass. What makes the Sacrament a means of grace is the active presence of the crucified and risen Lord. In the Sacrament he renews his covenant with his church, incorporates his disciples of all time in a communion with himself, and bestows on them "the forgiveness of sins, life, and salvation." [24]

Everything the Reformation says about Word and Sacrament as means of grace is directly and inseparably joined with the confession of justification by faith alone. As we have already seen, "justification by faith alone" is equivalent to "through Christ alone." Justification by faith is the work Christ continually performs in his church, and this continuing work of redemption takes place through the Word and the Sacrament as means of grace.

These facts shed light on the historical and ideological relationships of the Reformation liturgy. If everything said about "the means of grace" has its background and its motivation in the fact that the living Lord is effectively present in these means and makes the people of the new covenant participants in the fulness of salvation, the Reformation's opposition to the liturgical development during the Middle Ages is clearly seen. The question is then not only about that practice of the sacrifice of the Mass which was the primary object of attack, but in general the whole passion piety cult with its practices which were characteristic of

---

[24] Aulén, *Eucharist and Sacrifice*, pp. 90ff.

the later Middle Ages. We look in vain in the Reformation for anything that would correspond to that sentimental sympathy with and pity for the suffering Christ which was characteristic of this type of piety. There is nothing more misleading than Bouyer's claim that the Protestant "Mass" was characterized by "an absorbing contemplation of Our Lord in His passion only, to the total exclusion of any thought of His resurrection." [25] On the contrary, the characteristic view is precisely the synoptic view of cross and resurrection. The reconciling act of the cross is fulfilled, final, and for ever valid. The work of the risen and living Lord continues through the means of grace of the Word and the sacraments. This work of Christ is "justification." Everything said about justification by faith alone would be meaningless if it were separated from this context, and if "justification" were to be something else than precisely the fact that the living Lord now, here in the present, realizes his once-for-all completed work of reconciliation.

This central aspect of what happens in the liturgy obviously testifies to a connection with the primitive and ancient church. The Reformation liturgy is not a reproduction of the liturgy of that time. Besides, in the matter of ritual the Reformation had no more of a set and uniform liturgy than the primitive and ancient church. The Reformation rituals manifested considerable variations. No single one was sanctioned as *the* Reformation ritual. Nevertheless liturgical endeavors were supported by some conspicuously mutual interests, especially the desire to guard the conception of the means of grace. This interest explains the Reformation's negative attitude toward the Canon of the Roman Mass, its positive attitude toward the fundamental core of the liturgical tradition, and its creative impulses. The same interest explains the concern that the gospel, "the greatest treasure of the church," be proclaimed clearly and intelligibly in the language of the people, and also the concern for the active participation of the congregation in the communion and in the worship service in general. In this latter respect hymn singing came to play a very significant part. What ties this Reformation liturgy to the Bible and the ancient church is primarily the fundamental motif

[25] Bouyer, *Piety*, p. 42.

155

in the worship service: fellowship with the living Lord, participation in the salvation he has won and now bestows through the means of grace, and response to this act of the Lord in the church's common confession, prayer, and praise.

But even though the intentions of the Reformation liturgy stood in harmony with the liturgy of the church as this grew up on the basis of the Bible and in the spirit of the ancient church, this liturgical direction has not always been followed in post-Reformation history. To be sure, it has never disappeared, but it has had to contend with various tendencies which threatened to obscure its meaning. When Bouyer describes the "Protestant" worship service as concentrated one-sidedly around the pulpit, or when he somewhat caustically says that when the Protestant seeks nourishment for his faith, he finds it "only in the form of a total subjection to all the peculiarities, the momentary idiosyncrasies, of his minister's personal devotion," [26] it cannot be denied that there is some substantial foundation for this description, even in case of those churches which are associated with the reformation stemming from Luther. The difference, as over against the Reformation, lay in the fact that the worship service became a one-sided service of preaching and that the sacraments were unduly neglected. This development was based on the assumption that there was some kind of rivalry between the spoken Word and the Sacrament, a conception entirely foreign to the Reformation. This could lead to a kind of apotheosis of the sermon, which overlooked or did not reckon with the dangers inherent in the fact that here "the Word" comes in the form of a human witness. Such an apotheosis of the sermon would in reality imply that the minister "controls" the Word; or, in other words, his relationship to the Word would be kindred to that of the Roman priest to the Sacrament. Not all preaching is, in Paul's words, "the preaching of Christ" (Rom. 10:17). The difference, as over against the Reformation, also appeared in the interpretation of the Lord's Supper in that the Lord's Supper became one-sidedly connected with the passion of Christ, and at the same time was understood in an exclusively individualistic

---

[26] Bouyer, *Spirit*, p. 216.

manner.[27] The criticism Bouyer levels against the Reformation is at any rate somewhat relevant to what has since appeared in the churches of the Reformation. But such changes and reinterpretations cannot be directly derived from the Reformation, any more than, for example, Medieval passion piety can be derived from the patristic liturgy. Here other factors have been at work. In regard to the interpretation of the Lord's Supper we could point in part to the development of the doctrine of the Atonement in Orthodoxy and in part to the aftereffects of Medieval passion piety, which in various ways, especially through Pietism, exercised an influence in the Reformation churches. It may then be established that the Reformation formulations did not provide an effective guarantee against changes of this kind any more than Chalcedon, for instance, constituted an effective protection for its fundamental christological view. But this is something else than blaming the Reformation for ideas which are foreign to it. A strong attestation of the real position of the Reformation is the fact that study of the meaning of the Reformation, which has to such a great extent characterized evangelical theology in this century, has also contributed to a liturgical renewal in sharp contrast to the liturgical decadence of the nineteenth century and which consciously ties in with Reformation and early Christian motifs.

But even though there actually is in some essential respects a greater affinity between the Reformation and modern Roman strivings toward a liturgical renaissance than Bouyer recognized and admitted, the antithesis between them nevertheless appears clear and evident. We are reminded that, according to Bouyer, there has often been in modern Catholicism an "overemphasis" on the Real Presence, and that by this he means a one-sided emphasis on the elements of the Lord's Supper. This one-sidedness was to be opposed through an appeal to the presence of Christ in the hierarchy and the church. We are interested primarily in what is said about the presence of Christ in the hierarchy. *This* presence is really so to say primary. All other presence of Christ is derived from and dependent on this one. It is in turn dependent on the apostolic succession according to the

[27] Aulén. *Eucharist and Sacrifice,* pp. 102ff.

order of the Roman church. "Only a man who has validly received the divine commission through the apostolic succession
can validly perform the Eucharist. Any other Eucharist is empty
of reality, because empty of significance." [28]

It is not surprising that discussion with the "Protestants" ar-
rives at this point. We have seen the same development in other
contexts. Whatever the question at issue might be, the hierarchy
is finally brought into the picture. All roads lead to this point.
Here the final decisions are made whether it be in regard to
doctrine, authority (*potestas*), or, as in this case, liturgy.

In regard to liturgy the accusation against "Protestantism" is
that it leads to a tragic alternative: either magic or—so to speak
—going through the motions but not producing anything. The
"Protestant" Reformers "and especially Luther" had, it is said,
a correct intention when they maintained that Word and Sacrament cannot be separated, and that "the Word comes first" insofar as it works "through the sacraments." "But the reformers
were wrong in so far as they did not see that the true Word of
God is not present merely because someone repeats the material
letter of it, but because God himself is present in His Son, His
Son who is present in those men whom He has sent just as He
has been sent by the Father." When the Protestants either in
general would not recognize any kind of ordination, or else refused
"to acknowledge in ordination a real transmission of a sacred
power," the result was the tragic alternative mentioned above:
either the magical conception according to which valid sacraments
come into being simply by reason of the fact that somebody—
indeed anybody whatsoever—reads the Words of Institution over
the bread and wine, a view that can be traced in decadent
nominalism, *or* the view that the sacrament is invalid and devoid
of meaning.[29] The "alternative" proposed here is certainly only
apparent. The real situation, according to this criticism, is that
the Protestant sacrament is void of content and meaning.

The result of this reasoning is the following. "The Word" is
the Word of God only when it is pronounced by a priest rightly
ordained according to the Roman order. The Sacrament has no

[28] Bouyer, *Piety*, p. 146.
[29] *Ibid.*, pp. 149-50.

validity, it is meaningless, unless this presupposition obtains. Finally, we can speak in various ways about the presence of Christ. But this presence is primarily a presence in the hierarchy. If Christ is not present there, he is not present at all, either in Word or Sacrament. Thus the question of *order* comes to the front. It will be considered in the next section.

The question we raised was: What does the primacy of Scripture imply for the worship life of the church, the liturgy? It might appear that we have practically forgotten this question in our discussion with Bouyer. In reality we have had it in mind all the time. We are now able to answer it by summarizing a few fundamental points of view from our previous discussion. We cannot enter on a detailed discussion, but can only present a few principal guide lines.

Worship life within the Christian church presents rich and manifold "traditions." In and by itself this is nothing contrary to the normative character of Scripture. The Bible does not provide us with a uniform and firmly fixed order of service. The normative character of Scripture does not mean uniformity. The worship life of the church down through the ages has never been developed as a copy of biblical and early Christian practice. But this does not mean that the Bible does not furnish clear directives. Unquestionably it does. It posits its definite questions to and its definitive demands on all Christian worship life. It does so especially in two respects: in regard to worship's content and in regard to its character or quality.

The Bible does not leave us in uncertainty in regard to the content of Christian worship. It is said of the early church that "they devoted themselves to the apostles' teaching and fellowship, to the breaking of bread and the prayers" (Acts 2:42). Other biblical texts speak also about confession and songs of praise as essential elements in worship. The message, the apostolic proclamation, and the Lord's Supper, together with confession, prayer, and hymns of praise on the part of the congregation, appear as the central content in the worship of the early church and its "fraternal fellowship." Here we can refrain from entering on any detailed discussion of the historical-exegetical problems connected with the development and construction of the worship service in the earliest Christian church. In this connection it is sufficient to emphasize that the proclamation of the message was a self-evident presupposition of the growth and life of the church, and that, as all later biblical research has forcefully underscored, the Lord's Supper was the given center of Christian fellowship. These facts present definite questions to and demands upon all Christian communions.

The meaning of these demands, however, appear most clearly only when we consider the directives which Scripture presents in regard to the quality of worship. The most essential factor is that *synoptic view* of cross and resurrection which characterizes biblical worship life, which appeared so prominently during the days of the ancient church, and which undeniably experienced a renaissance during the Reformation, but which has been so often obscured in later times even within the reformed churches. Both preaching and the celebration of the Lord's Supper must be characterized by this synoptic view. Both derive their quality from the fact that the work of reconciliation has been perfected once for all on the cross, and that Christ as the living Lord ever renews his redemptive act in his church. Through this and this alone the proclamation of the Word and the sacraments of the Lord's Supper and Baptism become those *means of grace* which create and sustain the church of Christ on earth. Through this fact the confession of the congregation, its confession of sin and its confession of faith, its prayers and its praise, are established, made alive, and given their real character.

16. *ORDO*

The question of order has played a prominent role in ecumenical deliberations. The different conceptions presented revealed special and apparently insurmountable divisions between the various communions. The chief subject of discussion has been the episcopal conception of the church and "apostolic succession." As we have already seen, such claims may be interpreted in various ways both in regard to motivation and conclusions. We find the most radical claim concerning the nature of a "valid" order in the Roman church. Time and again we noted how in the last analysis various problems are referred back to "the hierarchy" and there find their solution. We have seen that Roman theologians may be highly critical of Roman tradition in many respects, but in reference to the hierarchy and its fundamental significance for the churches they stand firmly in the Roman tradition as this has been developed through the centuries and recently has been defined by the dogma of infallibility. A fundamental and distinctive mark of the church is the hierarchy which is validly ordained in the unbroken apostolic succession, and which stands in common with the Pope and under his infallible authority.

It has been said about the "Lutheran" churches that they pay very little attention to order. They are said to have concentrated their interest in doctrine to such an extent that nothing has been left for the problems of church order. When we look at the history of these churches, it cannot be denied that there are reasons for making this claim. But, on the other hand, it cannot be denied that these churches from the very beginning maintained the necessity of a ministry of the Word and the sacraments, and that this ministry was conceived of as a divine commission, which thus existed *jure divino*. These very facts demand that we define the fundamental standpoint of the Lutheran Reformation. We could ask: does the office of the ministry belong among the constitutive factors of the church, and, if so, in what sense?

If we look at Article VII of the Augsburg Confession, it might seem that the office of the ministry does not belong to the *notae* of the church. The article states, "For the true unity of the church it is enough to agree concerning the teaching of the Gospel and the administration of the sacraments." The office of the ministry is not mentioned in this connection. The conclusion has often been drawn that the office of the ministry does not belong to the constitutive factors of the church, and this conclusion has undoubtedly helped to minimize interest in the order of the church. Forgotten is the fact that Article V immediately preceding has just spoken of how the office of teaching the gospel and administering the sacraments was instituted, and of how this institution was declared to be necessary in the following words: "For, through the Word and sacraments, as through instruments, the Holy Spirit is given, and the Holy Spirit produces faith, where and when it pleases God, in those who hear the Gospel." This is not simply a matter of convenience. The office of the ministry is inseparably connected with the means of grace and a necessary instrument in their service. In other words, it exists *jure divino*. It is the gift of Christ. In Luther's words, it is "a service that comes *from* Christ, not to Christ, and which comes *to* us, not from us."

If then the office of the ministry is an essential and necessary function in the church and is founded on a divine commission, it is obviously something constitutive for the church. Since this is the case, we might ask why Lutheranism has been reluctant to include order among the "marks" of the church. Two explanations may be offered. In the first place, they did not want to set the office of the ministry on a par with the means of grace. They wanted to emphasize its position as a servant to the Word and the sacraments. In the second place, they did not want to associate the office of the ministry with any definite form of consecration or with any specifically defined church constitution. The Lutheran Reformation differentiates itself, therefore, both from Rome with its theory of succession and its attachment of the ministry to the Pope, and from the Reformed theory that the church's constitution was to be regulated by the Bible, and that biblical church order was equivalent to the "presbyterian." What is rejected is *not* the idea that the office of the ministry of the Word and the sacraments belongs to the constitution of the church, but the assertion that in order to function validly it must be founded on ordination in the Roman succession under the authority of the Pope, and the assumption that the Bible is supposed to provide fixed and definite rules for the form of church order.

Within Lutheran churches the constitutional order is not uniformly organized. The confessional writings of the Reformation bear witness to the fact that the Reformers not only had nothing against the episcopal office, but wanted to retain it if possible. In Germany it became impossible. The ordination of new pastors had to be undertaken without the assistance of the bishops. In Scandinavia episcopacy was retained, and in the Swedish church the apostolic succession was preserved. The office of bishop is

162

not found in American Lutheranism. Even though different forms of order thus appear among these churches from the beginning it has been fully agreed that he who is to administer the ministerial office of Word and sacrament must be *rite vocatus*. They are therefore agreed that the divine commission is bestowed by the church through those who are authorized to do so. In regard to the attitude of Lutherans toward the episcopal office we may make two remarks: first, where the episcopal office is lacking a substitute office is constituted; and, second, on the European continent there is an increasing return to the episcopal office, a trend which betokens a growing appreciation of the significance of this office.

The fact that order has taken different forms in the family of Lutheran churches has not constituted a barrier to church fellowship. The decisive point here is that the "validity" of the means of grace has not been made dependent on one or the other of the prevailing types of order. The episcopal office, with or without "unbroken" succession, may be treasured for various reasons, but not because it guarantees the effectiveness of the means of grace. The Word and the Sacrament do not lose their power if this is omitted. They have their validity in themselves. It is not the office of the ministry that makes the Word a word of God and makes the Sacrament effective, but rather the fact that Christ and the Spirit are active in the Word, and that the living Christ acts in the sacraments instituted by him, and that he, in reference to the Lord's Supper, has bound his saving presence to the celebration of the sacrament of bread and wine in his church. Bouyer's alternative noted above, according to which "Protestant" celebration of the Lord's Supper is either magical or empty, has therefore no application at all. That the sacrament is an effective means of grace depends on the fact that Christ fulfils his promise to meet his disciples in the bread and wine of the Holy Supper, and thus takes them into communion with himself to share in the salvation he has procured. The office of the ministry is nothing more than an instrument functioning in the service of Word and Sacrament, but also nothing less. It is not the office of the ministry that makes the means of grace a means of grace, but rather it is the means of grace which enables the ministry to function according to the commission and authority of Christ. Everything is dependent on the fact that the means of grace have their validity and power in themselves, or rather through Christ, because through them the living Lord carries on his redemptive work in his church. How completely dominant and decisive this view of the matter is may be seen in the really radical words against "the Donatists" in Article VIII of the Augsburg Confession: "Both the sacraments and the Word are effectual by reason of the institution and commandment of Christ even if they are administered by evil men." It is unnecessary to say that the statement was made not in order to reduce the personal demands which must be made of those who are to serve as pastors in the church of Christ, but exclusively in order to maintain the priority of the means of grace, their *majestas materiae,* in reference to the office of the ministry.

Against the background of what we have just said the Roman conception of the "hierarchy" appears very clearly. The difference appears first and foremost in the fact that the validity of the means of grace is completely dependent on the office of the ministry as this has been developed and fixed according to Roman order. Its validity demands ordination in the unbroken apostolic succession and an attitude of obedience to papal authority. Where these conditions are not fulfilled, there is no valid ministry nor any effective means of grace. Even if Rome were to acknowledge that independently of Rome there are pastors ordained in an unbroken apostolic succession, this fact would not result in a recognition of the legitimacy of this office since fellowship with the Pope is lacking. Thus Rome has refused to recognize the office of the ministry in the Anglican church, and Rome would no doubt take the same negative view toward the Swedish church. Rome's claim, that the Roman church is the only true church, is simply a natural result of its position. If the validity and effectiveness of the means of grace are dependent on a valid hierarchy in the Roman sense, and if the means of grace otherwise cease to be effective, inevitably the church becomes identical with the Roman church. This must be the attitude in principle. The fact that in view of obvious realities they may be compelled to make certain modifications is quite a different matter.

The reason why the effectiveness of the means of grace are made dependent on the hierarchy is that the "divine powers," the *"pouvoirs apostoliques"* (Congar), are mediated in ordination. If this power is really to be transmitted, ordination must take place within the unbroken apostolic succession. Power is transferred through that line which runs from the apostles to the present time. Just as electrical power ceases to function when the line is cut, thus also the power of the hierarchy would cease if the succession were broken at any one point. Through this power the means of grace receive their validity and effectiveness. The ordained priest receives the power to bring forth "the sacrifice for the living and the dead" in the Mass. In an encyclical of 1935 Pius XI wrote: "Herein appears clearly the inexpressible greatness of the Catholic office of the priesthood, that it has authority over the Body of Christ, because in the name of the divine Redeemer it makes his body present on our altars and offers it as an acceptable sacrifice to the eternal and divine majesty." [30]

It may be illuminating in this connection to remind ourselves of Bouyer's argumentation about the presence of Christ. He seeks to maintain that the presence attached to the elements of the Lord's Supper has sometimes been overemphasized. It is obvious that his criticism is intended to underscore the *active* presence of Christ, and that it is part of his endeavor to emphasize that the Crucified is at the same time the risen and living Lord in opposition to a one-sided passion piety. It is also obvious that this emphasis must result in a greater stress on the presence of Christ in his church. Bouyer indeed speaks about this, but only after he has heavily underscored the special presence of Christ in the hierarchy. The argument runs that this presence, mediated through the succession, is the *primary* condition for all other presence of Christ. Christ is present in the elements only because "he is present in that man" who celebrates the Mass. When thereupon the presence of Christ in the church is realized in and through the Eucharist, this presence, too, is derived from the presence localized in the hierarchy through the succession.

The unbroken succession, therefore, is the foundation on which

[30] Persson, "Vad är romerskt," *loc. cit.*, pp. 18-19.

"the hierarchical constitution of the Church," and the presence of Christ, rests. But in order for the office of the ministry to be valid it must stand in fellowship with the Pope and under his authority. According to the dogma of 1870 this authority is infallible when the Pope *ex cathedra* issues regulations for the faith and life of the church. The Pope has infallibility as the successor to Peter, the prince of the apostles, and as the vicar of Christ. No ecclesiastical departments need to be consulted. The Pope issues his decrees *ex sese*.

On the basis of this view of the fulness of papal power it is self-evident that the Roman church should be designated as the only true church. No other church is endowed with infallible leadership like this. It also becomes self-evident that the office of the ministry must be obedient to the papal authority. Only in this way can there be any guarantee that the hierarchy will be given the guidance it needs to perform its task.

It is unnecessary to go into details regarding the consequences of the dogma of infallibility. The matter has been touched upon previously in different connections. We have pointed out that through this dogma papal authority has been set free from the authority of the Bible and from continuity with the ancient traditions of the church. Reverence for the Mother of Jesus has indeed a biblical anchorage which is far from being recognized in the churches of the Reformation. But the two Marian dogmas lack any biblical justification and besides they stand in opposition to the tradition of the ancient church.

The presentation we have given of the Reformation conception of order and that of the Roman church pointed out the difference between them. This difference does not concern the divine institution and commission of the office of the ministry, nor its necessity for the life of the church. The difference appears especially at three points. In the first place, it appears in the fact that the validity and effectiveness of the means of grace are made dependent on a specific form of ordination in which the priest receives episcopal consecration in "the unbroken apostolic succession." Only through this consecration can he become a partaker of that "divine power" which is a necessary condition if the means of grace are to function effectively as means of grace. In the second place, it appears in the fact that the presence of Christ is conceived of primarily as a presence in the hierarchy, and that all other presence of Christ is derived from this. Over against this claim stands the conception according to which Christ has tied his presence in the church to the means of grace—the Word and the sacraments—through which he realizes his redemptive work ever anew. The ministry of the church has been given the specific task of administering the means of grace. But Christ's presence and fellowship with those he has accepted into his service is not of another character nor does it have any other foundation than that which applies to all other members of the church. Finally, the difference appears in the alleged infallibility ascribed to the leadership of the church as represented in the papal power. Christ's promise of the guidance of the Spirit, to which they refer, certainly is steadfast. But when the guidance of the Spirit is attached to a private individual, it appears as a usurpation which has no foundation in the promise of Christ. The Spirit is tied to Christ and his word, not to the Pope or to any ecclesiastical authority. The theories about the special presence of Christ in the hierarchy and the identification of the guidance of the Spirit with the leadership of the Pope obscure and overshadow the supremacy of Christ and the Spirit in all the circumstances of life in the church.

Our comparison of the Roman and the Reformation conceptions of order is intended to illuminate certain controversial questions about the office of the ministry that have appeared in ecumenical conversations. This applies to the first of the points discussed above. The two others, the theses concerning Christ's special and primary presence in the hierarchy and the infallibility concentrated in the papal power, are specifically Roman, and have consequently had no advocates within those communions which participate in ecumenical deliberations. But the questions about episcopal constitution of the church and of the apostolic succession have played an exceedingly prominent part. In this respect, as we well know, various antitheses have appeared. In view of this fact it is important to determine if and when these antitheses have had reference to essential characteristics.

These antitheses would obviously be of fundamental character if a certain definite church order were to be regarded as the only biblically valid one. It is obvious that such an attitude is completely foreign to the Lutheran Reformation. This is clear not merely because different orders, both episcopal and nonepiscopal, are found within Lutheran churches. That at the time of the Reformation the episcopal office was not preserved in Germany was not due, as we have seen, to any prejudice against the office on the part of the Reformers. When Luther, in spite of all his criticism, speaks of the Roman church as a "holy" church, he points not only to the fact that the gospel, Baptism, and the Lord's Supper are found there, but also to "the ecclesiastical offices" (cf. above, p. 76). His criticism against the bishops and the Pope is directed not against the office as such, but against its attitude toward the gospel which is "the greatest treasure of the church." That ordination of priests came to be carried out without the assistance of bishops was not due to any desire on the part of the Reformers. It took place against their wishes and of necessity because of the opposition of the bishops of the time.

The Calvinistic Reformation assumed from the beginning a different position insofar as it maintained the "presbyterian" order as the only biblical one. Later churches of congregational type have argued in the same way about their form of order. This has not prevented the Hungarian Reformed church from having bishops, nor the Methodist church which developed within the Reformed tradition. When we review the modern ecumenical discussions about the office of the ministry, we do not in general find very much of the original Reformed and Congregational conceptions, according to which their respective orders were supposed to be the only biblically legitimate ones. The strongest attestation of how this biblicistic argumentation has more or less faded is to be found in the mergers and merger negotiations between churches which constitute such a marked feature of modern church history. In this connection it is sufficient to refer to the Church of South India, which includes Anglicans, Presbyterians, Methodists, and Congregationalists, and to the present negotiations between the Church of England and the Church of Scotland.

When we look at this kind of negotiations, which is taking

place at the present time in various areas of Christendom, the important thing is not that one or several communions are to be absorbed by another, but rather that those who have been separated now are to unite. In regard to the question of church order we may note that both presbyterian and congregational elements have been preserved in the episcopal Church of South India. But the idea that a presbyterian or congregational church order is the only biblically legitimate order is not held any longer. What then is the Anglican position? An inflexible condition for Anglican participation was that the "historic episcopate" was to be preserved in the new united church. Our interest is not in the fact that such a condition was insisted on; a church can of course put up any kind of conditions it deems necessary for its voluntary participation in a union. What we are especially interested in is *how the matter was justified*. The motivation has not been, and could not be, biblicistic. Undoubtedly different motives have worked together, above all the strong tradition in the history of Christianity, but also various matters of expediency. These factors are legitimate and well worth attention. There is, however, one justification which could not have been invoked, and which, if it had been, would have closed the door to all negotiations, namely, the conception which makes the validity and effectiveness of the means of grace dependent on episcopal ordination in the "apostolic succession." We cannot begin merger negotiations by unchurching the churches with whom we intend to unite.

Here we come to the controversial point which undoubtedly is of a fundamental nature. The antithesis in principle in the area of church order arises because, and only because, the validity and effectiveness of the means of grace are made dependent on episcopal ordination with "apostolic succession." No matter how many other strong motives we cite in favor of the episcopal order and no matter how highly we treasure the continuity of the succession, all this does not result in any fundamental antithesis, provided we do not draw the *dogmatic* conclusion that the validity and effectiveness of the means of grace depend on this specific form of the office of the ministry. As soon as this is done, the antithesis becomes fundamental. The reason for this is perfectly

169

clear. Such a limitation of that power which the means of grace possess in themselves means in reality nothing less than a limitation of the sovereignty of Christ. Christ is not and cannot be tied down to any one form of ordination to the ministerial office.

In addition to what has been said we add a marginal note here in reference to the position of the Anglican church. The Church of England, whose Lambeth Conference of 1930 encouraged the attempts toward union in South India, has not yet established full communion with the united Church of South India. The Lambeth Conference of 1948 for the time being assumed a wait-and-see attitude because, it was said, "a strong minority" was critical of the union established in 1947. This attitude indicates the conflicting theories of the ministry to be found within the Anglican church. The conflict is concerned with the question of whether such dogmatic conclusions as we have discussed above should be derived from the theory of the office of the ministry.[31]

We have previously considered the traditions of the various churches in reference to order. It remains now to discuss how these traditions are related to what the Bible has to say about the order of the church. What does a reference to Scripture as norm mean in this case? To what extent can we speak of directives given in Scripture?

In recent times there has been a lively interest in the church order of the Bible. Modern biblical studies within the various confessions have emphasized the great part which the problems of "organization" played even in the early church, as we can see in the New Testament writings. In the early church the word "priest" itself was not used in the sense of a special office in the service of the *ecclesia*. When this term is used, it refers to all the members of the church. To be a member in the church of Christ means to belong to "a chosen race, a royal priesthood" (I Pet. 2:9). Christ has "made us a kingdom, priests to his

[31] In regard to the attitude of the 1958 Lambeth Conference the following statement from an article in *The Ecumenical Review* might be added. "Obviously the Anglican Communion's continued study of the life of the Church of South India and its conversation with this church during the last ten years have helped Lambeth's Committee to understand more sympathetically than before some of the problems that any attempt at church union is likely to involve" (*The Ecumenical Review*, 1959, p. 182).

God and Father" (Rev. 1:6). When the word priest is used here as a designation of membership in the church of Christ, it means full and complete participation in the redemptive riches which belonged to the new people of God in the new covenant. This "priesthood" was also "to offer spiritual sacrifices acceptable to God through Jesus Christ" (I Pet. 2:5; cf. Rom. 12:1). The Bible does not divide the church into an active and a passive part. The activity belongs to the church as a whole. But this "universal priesthood," as it came to be known later in the history of Christianity, did not mean that in the early church there were no *special* offices, services, and commissions. The apostolic office was the original starting point. When the church grew and new congregations were organized, there followed new offices: deacons, presbyters, and bishops, together with a number of other services and commissions. It is sufficent in this case to refer to the "varieties of gifts" of which Paul speaks in I Corinthians 12.

The church of Easter and Pentecost was a concrete entity. It expanded and grew through the missionary activity of the apostles and their fellow workers. From the very beginning it had not only a definite message and specific worship but also an organization. The New Testament has much to say about this. But we look in vain in the Bible for any unified and established church order which might serve as a regulation and law for subsequent ages. For this reason alone none of the subsequent church orders that we find later in the history of Christianity can claim that they are the only legitimately biblical ones.

In a book with the title, *Glaube und Leben der Urgemeinde,* which deals with the first seven chapters of Acts, Bo Reicke showed how organizational patterns, which later went their separate ways, existed together in union in the early church. His investigation deals with the selection of an apostle in chap. 1 and the appointment of the deacons in chap. 6. In the selection of an apostle we find: 1) a monarchical or episcopal element in the emphasis on the leadership of Peter; 2) an oligarchical or presbyterian element in the reference to the authority of the apostles; 3) a democratic or congregational element represented by the presence and consent of the congregation; 4) a theocratic element: the final decision is regarded as a divine decision. In a similar way at the appointment of the deacons there is a co-operative action between the apostles and the congregation. The choice of the congregation is sanctioned by the apostles as the highest authority, and the ones selected are thereafter consecrated to their service with prayer and the laying on of hands.[32]

These organizational proceedings and a number of others described in the apostolic letters show that later church orders may find points of contact with the Bible, but at the same time they show that none of them can cite the Bible as exclusive authority for its special order whether it be congregational, presbyterian, episcopal, or papal. None of these have any counterpart in the early church. The New Testament did not sanction any definite church order as the only legitimate one. We know that it did not take very long before the episcopal order appeared in the early church. In comparison no other order has had such a strong position in the tradition. But in the Bible there was as yet no distinction between the function of bishops and that of presbyters. The most we can say is that the "monarchical" episcopacy begins to appear faintly in the Pastoral Epistles. The papal order has also tried to claim biblical sanction in the reference to Peter as the leader of the apostles. That he held this leadership both among the apostles and in the church is unquestionable, but the Bible makes no suggestion that this "primacy" was to be perpetuated in a permanent institution, still less that it was to be transferred to the Bishop of Rome, and least of all that it implies any infallibility.

Although we can establish the fact that the Bible does not represent any definite church order, and that it cannot be used as a church law valid for all time, this does not mean that the Bible is not normative also in reference to order. It would be misleading to propose an alternative of this kind: *either* we must use the Bible as a church law valid for all time, *or* we must refrain from seeking in it any directive with reference to order in the church. In reality the Bible provides very clear directives. This has reference especially to what the Bible has to say about the office of the ministry as a divine institution and about its character, meaning, and purpose.

[32] Bo Reicke, *Glaube und Leben der Urgemeinde* (1957), pp. 21ff., 118ff.

The office of the ministry as an institution of the Lord is primarily connected with the apostolate. "As the Father has sent me, even so I send you" (John 20:21). "Go therefore and make disciples of all nations" (Matt. 28:19). But the divine commission given to the apostles is not restricted to them. It is a commission which through the apostles as intermediaries continues in the church, a continuing office in apostolic succession. It is, to be sure, not an apostolic office. The apostolate has a special position in comparison to all other offices in the church, especially for two reasons. In the first place, as the New Testament emphasizes several times, the apostles are "the witnesses of the resurrection." The new apostle who was elected in the place of Judas Iscariot was appointed to "become with us a witness to his resurrection" (Acts 1:22). In the second place, the message the apostles proclaimed is fundamental and normative for the message for all time. None of these functions can be repeated. No one can be witness to the resurrection *in the same sense* as the apostles. The message they proclaimed was given *once for all* and cannot be changed. But precisely because this apostolic message is normative for all time, the continuity is preserved. The office which continues in the church is not an office of apostles, but *an apostolic office* nonetheless. It has a divine commission just like the apostles. It is an office *jure divino,* or rather, *gratia divina.* It is not a matter of expediency, or of something desirable according to changing situations, or else of something that could be eliminated. As a commission from the Lord it is something which belongs to the constitution of the church. That it is mediated through the church does not in any way nullify its character as a commission by the Lord himself. It has sometimes been discussed whether the commission should be regarded as a commission from the church *or* from the Lord, but this is an alternative completely foreign to the New Testament. Such a proposition considers only a sociological aspect of the church and becomes therefore incompatible with the Bible's religious view of the church as "the Body of Christ" and of Christ as the Lord of the church. If Christ is the church's *Kyrios,* the commission mediated through the church is at the same time a direct commission from the

173

Lord. The alternative mentioned above is meaningless. The commission from the church would not be a commission from the church if it were not a commission from that Lord who is "the Head" of the church.

In the biblical view, therefore, the office of the ministry in the church is a divine institution. But that is not all. The Bible also gives clear directives about the character and purpose of the office. Its character is first of all that of a *shepherd office*. "Tend the flock of God that is your charge" (I Pet. 5:2; cf. John 21:15 ff.). The shepherd office receives its character from the fact that, in the first place, it is altogether an office of service, and, in the second place, it has been endowed by the Lord with power and authority. It is never a question of anything else but service—being a servant of the church by being "servants of Christ and stewards of the mysteries of God" (I Cor. 4:1). But the servant is equipped with authority from the Lord, as this appears in the words concerning the power of the keys (Matt. 18:18; cf. 16:19 and John 20:22-23). The commission of the Lord is a necessary condition for carrying out the duties of the office. But the authority in question here is not attached to the servants themselves. It is not based on anything of their own. Its foundation lies in the Lord whom they serve and in the means, the Word of God and the sacraments, which he permits them to administer. They possess, therefore, no superiority over the rest of the members of the church, nor does the office assume any kind of a mediating position which would obscure or weaken its immediate relationship to Christ. As Paul tells the Corinthians, "Not that we lord it over your faith; we work with you for your joy" (II Cor. 1:24). Nor is it a matter of dividing the church into an active and a passive part. All its members are called to activity and service, but certain members have been called to and installed in a *special* service in the church.

When Christ continues and realizes his redemptive work in his church, he uses the servants of the Word and the sacraments as his instruments. Thus Paul says, "we are ambassadors for Christ." In this sense we could say that these servants "represent" Christ. But this expression, used and discussed in modern times, is not biblical, and it can too easily be interpreted in a misleading and dangerous way. This happens as soon as we forget or turn away from the idea of "the Real Presence" of Christ in Word and Sacrament. The presence, the Real Presence, is more than a representation. The presence of Christ is not some special presence *in* the servants of the Word and the sacraments. They are nothing but instruments. The presence of Christ does not depend on the power and authority of the priest, but only on the promise of Christ and on his *own* power.

The biblical view of the office of the ministry in the church directs its questions to all the church communions. It can be corrupted in various ways. This can be done through an objectivism which in one way or another mechanizes the means of grace. This has happened, to be sure, not only in the Roman church in regard to the sacraments, but also in the Protestant communions, here especially in regard to the Word as a means of grace. A corruption takes place also when the office of the ministry is conceived of from a subjective point of view, where the emphasis is placed on personal piety and the task is to foster and increase this further. In both cases those who were to be servants of the means of grace assume authority over them. In both cases "the office of the ministry" becomes primary in reference to the Word or the sacraments. That *majestas materiae* which the means of grace possess in themselves, or rather through Christ, has been obscured. In this connection we must not forget how foreign it is to the Bible to divide the church into an active and a passive part—how far the Bible is, in other words, from all clericalism. The question the Bible poses is surely directed to *all* church communions.

In the Bible we find the office of the ministry under different names and differentiations, which, however, are not firmly separated from one another. The biblical word for "the office of the ministry" is *diakonia* (II Cor. 4:1). The Swedish word *ämbete* (office) easily acquires a bureaucratic connotation, which is completely foreign to the biblical *diakonia*. The history of the church indicates that bureaucracy is one of the dangers to which "the office of the ministry" is subject. Sad to say, "Lutheranism" can tell us a great deal about this. From the biblical point of view the essential element is that the office is an office in the congregation. Its apostolic character depends not only on the fact that the office is mediated through the apostles, and is therefore an office in the apostolic succession, but also and above all on the nature and purpose of the office. It is a *shepherd office,* the primary function of which is to care for "the flock of God." This care may assume many forms. When the Bible speaks of "varieties of gifts" and services, it presents demands which have not become any less insistent in modern times. But the great variety is brought together and united in the one fact that always and everywhere the purpose of the office is to serve as an instrument for God's holy Word and the holy sacraments.

In the first chapter we were reminded of a statement by Florovsky about the office of the ministry in the church. He emphasized that in the Orthodox church a definite order, the episcopal, belongs to "Christian dogma," but he added that the question of the ministerial office is concerned primarily with *its sacramental character.* Such a diagnosis certainly has biblical support if the term "sacramental" is conceived—as by Florovsky —in an eschatological sense. The gospel and the sacraments served by the office of the ministry mean that the *eschaton,* that which is not of this world, encounters us in the midst of this world as the decisive, redemptive power, and at the same time comes as an anticipation and an earnest of the final consummation.

CHAPTER 5

CATHOLICITY

17. *THE NAME*

Two church communions designate themselves as "catholic." The Roman church uses the name *ecclesia catholica* interchangeably or together with *ecclesia romana*. The Old Catholic Church which broke away from Rome during the nineteenth century also uses the name catholic. No other communion has adopted this name for itself. The Eastern church indeed emphasizes its catholicity, but it prefers to call itself the Orthodox church. A fraction within the Anglican church designates itself as "Anglo-Catholic," but this term is not used of the Anglican church as a whole. Nathan Söderblom, who felt that it was wrong to reserve this name of honor in the confession of faith for the Roman church, suggested that what he called "the three principal divisions" of Christianity should be called Greek Catholic, Roman Catholic, and Evangelical Catholic. In popular usage in most of Christendom the word "catholic" has come to be used in a sense synonymous with Roman.

The long list of names of the numerous church communions which occur in popular usage are more or less dubious. They are either pretentious or one-sided, and therefore misleading. It is pretentious when a communion calls itself *the* orthodox church, or *the* catholic church. But it is certainly not less pretentious to designate the churches of the Reformation as evangelical, as if the gospel (evangel) were reserved for these churches. In the same way there is a danger in such names as Methodist and Baptist, which may seem to suggest that the real question is about the only true method of obtaining salvation or about the only true baptism. The name Presbyterian, which makes a certain form of church order decisive, also presents a one-sided aspect.

The name Protestantism, too, which was forced upon the Reformation for the purpose of polemics, is exceedingly one-sided because it suggests that the essential element in the Reformation was its "negations." If possible, an even less felicitous name is Lutheran, which came into use against the wishes of the Reformer himself. Luther thought about personal names in the same way as Paul: "Were you baptized in the name of Paul?" (I Cor. 1:13). Finally there is a certain danger of another kind when the name of the church is connected with a certain country or people, as for instance the Swedish church, or the Church of England, and so on. In this case the name applies to churches which are more or less closely related to the state. Such a system presents both advantages and disadvantages like any other. But the danger is not only that to an outsider the church may appear to be a department of the state, but also and especially that the power of the state in one way or another may put undue constraint on the life and work of the church.

Similar critical remarks may be made about other names. All names are in reality unsatisfactory, which is not at all surprising. The names originated for the purpose of distinguishing the various communions from one another. They point therefore to the fragmentation of Christendom. Since this fragmentation is unsatisfactory, it is not surprising that the names used to call attention to this fact are also unsatisfactory. There is only one satisfactory and adequate name: the name of Christ himself.

In both of the ancient confessions of faith, the Apostles' and the Nicene, the designation catholic is given to the church of Christ: the Apostles' Creed—"the holy catholic Church," the Nicene—"one holy catholic and Apostolic Church." This term "catholic" presents its challenge to all church communions. We cannot join in the confession about the catholicity of the church without seeking to clarify the attitude of our own communion to the catholicity we confess. Indifference to this question would mean that we dismiss the confession as empty words. It is obvious that no communion which takes the content of the confession seriously can attach the catholicity of the church to any one specific communion. Catholicity is at any rate a concern for all of them.

Those church communions which participate in ecumenical deliberations cannot of course conceive of catholicity as a prerogative of the Roman church. On the contrary, however, in ecumenical discussions there is frequent reference to two "blocks" or types, the "Catholic" and the "Protestant," which stand over against each other. This means in reality that the specific names return again, so to speak, in a typologically camouflaged sense. Those communions which did not experience or who rejected the Reformation are then regarded as catholic, especially the Orthodox and the Roman churches, while the Protestant fold includes not only the churches of the original Reformation but also all others who since established themselves as independent churches. In reference to this line of thought the Anglican church likes to think of itself as a bridge between the two, as at the same time catholic and reformed. As a result there appear various tendencies within Anglicanism depending on whether the catholic or the reformed element is emphasized.

Everyone who has participated in ecumenical conversations knows what difficulties have come up on account of this division into two principal camps. The perplexity is easily explained. This schematic typology which is used has naturally introduced a certain irrational and irritating element into the conversations. The reason for this is not in itself the attempt to clarify the actual differences between communions. Such a clarification and an open and frank view of the differences is an indispensable presupposition if conversation between all the parties is to be fruitful. But this desirable clarification is in reality made unnecessarily more difficult by the schematic typology. It causes special difficulties because it puts a restraint on the material with which we have to work. The various communions are forced into a strait jacket which ties them down and hinders their free movement. In other words, this conception is entirely too static.

The attempt to divide Christianity into two blocks or principal types presupposes that there is considerable unity within each "block." In reality there are so many differences on *both* sides that we must question the propriety and the practicality of this popular division. In regard to the first block we may remind ourselves of the sharp antithesis between the organizational structure of the Orthodox church and the autocratic papal system, of how foreign the idea is to the Orthodox church that new dogmas may be proclaimed by an infallible papal authority, and of the wide difference between the Orthodox and the Roman both in regard to worship life and their conceptions of the church in general. Both of these communions make incontestable claims to represent a true catholicity, *the* true catholicity, but this obviously involves two different kinds of catholicity.

If we cannot, therefore, speak of a catholic "block" without forcing them into one form, it is even more clearly impossible to put a common stamp on all the communions which are designated as "Protestant." We need hardly say that the differences here are so great and deep that to speak of a common type becomes in reality meaningless. The former Bishop of South India, Lesslie Newbigin, has suggested that the traditional twofold division should be replaced by a division into three parts, that besides the "catholic" and the "Protestant" types there should be a third which he calls "Pentecostal." [1] Newbigin may have good reasons for introducing a third type like this. But I do not mention his suggestion in order to substitute a threefold for a twofold classification, but only as an example of the differences, not to say antitheses, to be found within what we call Protestantism. From an ecumenical point of view it cannot possibly be in the interest of ecumenical endeavor to make typological classifications of this kind. It has been rather well established that they confuse the deliberations and make them more difficult. As a rule the different communions react forcefully against any attempt to impose a category upon their own particular communion. They do not recognize its applicability to themselves. This is true both of "Catholic" attempts to describe the "Protestant" type and vice versa. To group together the different communions in this way and to incorporate them into different principal types leads in reality to insurmountable difficulties and violates the actual situation.

It is quite another matter to seek to clarify the relationship between different communions taken individually. K. E. Skyds-

[1] Gustaf Wingren, "Kyrkoordning och Enhet," in *Svensk teologisk kvartalskrift,* 1958, p. 273.

gaard has made just such an attempt in his instructive book, *One In Christ*.[2] In the subtitle of the original Danish work, *Forstaaelse af Forholdet mellem Katolicisme og Protestantisme* ["Toward an Understanding of the Relationship between Catholicism and Protestantism"], Skydsgaard indeed uses the terms Catholic and Protestant, but the investigation is concerned exclusively with the relationship between the Roman and Lutheran churches. It is made with full realization of the difficulties encountered even when the analysis is limited to only two communions. What gives special interest and liveliness to Skydsgaard's presentation is the fact that his point of view is not static. Skydsgaard underscores how unsatisfactory it would be to speak of the relationship between the two communions as a once-for-all stereotyped and fixed antithesis. Both communions are living churches.[3] Much has happened in both of them since the time of the Reformation, and much is happening today. The problems have changed. An analysis which does not take due account of this becomes necessarily misleading. In other words, the static point of view has been replaced by a dynamic one.

As we recall the statements of the Roman theologians we have considered in this book, it is obvious that they naturally maintain the catholicity of the Roman church. We saw how they do it. But it is just as obvious that their intensive attempts toward a liturgical renewal must be said to imply a striving to realize more adequately that catholicity which the Roman church possesses. I imagine that these Roman theologians would raise no objections against such a formulation. Departures from what a true liturgy means, which they so emphatically criticize, must be described as foreign to true catholicity. They represent an a-catholic element and constitute an indication that catholicity has been imperfectly realized.

This observation itself shows that the problem of catholicity and its real meaning cannot be solved by attaching catholicity to one communion or even to a group of them in contrast to others. Catholicity, in other words, is not a geographical but a qualitative conception of fundamental character. As catholicity places its

[2] *One in Christ* (Philadelphia: Muhlenberg, 1957).
[3] *Ibid.*, pp. 27ff.

questions and demands before the Roman communion, it confronts likewise all other communions, not least those who are usually referred to as Protestant. The Creed reminds us of this inescapable fact. Indeed it does not say, "we believe in one holy Protestant church," but "we believe in one holy catholic church." Our primary task, therefore, will be to seek to define what meaning the word catholicity has in the context of the Creed. Before we pass to an explication of this subject, we simply want to add that the question about their relationship to catholicity has been actualized in different ways within those communions which traditionally are not called catholic. The modern ecumenical movement has undoubtedly contributed to this development. But it would be quite wrong if we were to claim that it has been the only effective factor.

18. *THE MEANING OF CATHOLICITY*

According to the Nicene Creed the church is *one, holy, catholic,* and *apostolic.* Each of these attributes expresses something essential about the church of Christ. At the same time all four of them have grown together to constitute such a unity that attempts to differentiate them from one another are doomed to failure. In reality they speak, with different nuances to be sure, of one and the same thing. That this is the case depends, in the last analysis, on the fact that the confession of the unity, holiness, catholicity, and apostolicity of the church has its foundation in the confession of the *Kyrios* whose "Body" the church is. The unity of the church rests on the fact that Christ is its *Kyrios.* Unity is a unity "in Christ." The church is holy because in it Christ realizes his redemptive work. The same is true of the terms catholic and apostolic. The church is apostolic and the apostles are the norm for what happens in the church because the apostles are the chosen and authorized witnesses and messengers of Christ.

Catholicity, too, is entirely dependent on the fact that Christ is the Lord of the church. Perhaps it could be said that the meaning of catholicity does not appear as immediately as that of unity, holiness, and apostolicity. The interpretation of its meaning has varied. But two fundamental aspects inevitably come

182

to the fore: *universality* and *continuity*. The two are closely related and cannot be separated. The church could not be the universal church if it did not through the ages stand in unbroken relationship with the original church which had its origin in Christ, the church of Easter and Pentecost.

The universality of the church is one with the universality of the atonement of Christ. "God was in Christ reconciling the *world* to himself." As reconciliation was for the world as a whole, so also the dominion of the exalted and glorified Christ is universal. This is the background of the missionary injunction: "All authority in heaven and on earth has been given to me. Go therefore and make disciples of all nations." The work the living Lord performs in and through his church has a universal purpose. It does not recognize any human marks of distinction. It abolishes all human boundaries. It determines the character of the church. It gives the church universality. It is the very nature of the church to transgress boundaries and break them down. The church is not and cannot be an entity comprised, limited, confined, and isolated within itself. The church has a *dynamic* character. The catholicity of the church is an expression of the universal scope of Love's victorious act in Christ. It also expresses the fact that the God of creation and the God of redemption are one and the same.

But at the same time catholicity means continuity. Universality and continuity are inseparably connected. Without this union with continuity, boundary-transgressing universality would run the risk of becoming an undefined spiritualism. The continuity which characterizes the church of Christ, and must characterize it, is derived primarily from the fact that Christ and his Spirit unchangeably use the same means for the realization of salvation in the church, namely, the means of grace, the Word and the sacraments. In this way the church as a communion and congregation of saints preserves its specific character. It could be said with some justification that universality and continuity balance one another. Universality stands for the openness of the church; continuity, for its stability. It is precisely continuity that prevents a contourless dissolution, while universality prevents a narrow and cramped isolation.

183

We suggested above that all the various terms used in the Creed have something essential to say about the church, but that at the same time the several attributes are too interlaced to be separated one from the other. In view of what we have said about catholicity it is perfectly clear that it is intimately connected with unity and apostolicity. The universality of the church presupposes its unity. It is not accidental that the first syllable in unity and universality is the same. The connection between apostolicity and continuity is also obvious. But this connection does not mean that the term catholicity does not have its own purpose to fulfil.

The church of Christ *is* one, holy, catholic, and apostolic church, and it is so because Christ is its Lord and the church is his "Body." "In Christ" and through his continuing activity in it the church *possesses* unity, holiness, catholicity, and apostolicity. But at the same time there is nothing more obvious than the fact that the life and work of the church is defective in all of these respects. Such defects are nothing new. The New Testament bears witness to the fact that they have existed from the very beginning. The early church was not an "ideal church." The apostolic letters are filled with admonitions to walk worthy of the gospel of Christ. The apostles fought against schisms and heresies. In other words, they fought against tendencies within the church which were destructive to its unity, holiness, catholicity, and apostolicity. It has been the same all through the ages. The history of the church testifies abundantly to the appearance of schism, sin, narrow isolation, and heresies. All these defects are derived from the fact that the church is not only holy but also sinful, at once *sancta et peccatrix*. The members of the church are "holy" because and insofar as they have been incorporated through the redemptive work of Christ into the new fellowship of life in the new covenant which came with the new age of the resurrection. But at the same time, as long as they live under the conditions of life on earth, they are also sinful. Perfection does not belong to this life on earth. The honorific titles which the Creed gives to the church are, therefore, on the one hand, something the church actually possesses, but, on the other hand, something which must be realized anew in struggle against the destructive powers.

184

In the preceding we have pointed out that the church's claim to the honorific titles the Creed ascribes to it stands or falls on the fact that Christ is the Lord of the church, and that the church is his "Body." It is of highest importance to understand what the term "Body of Christ" means and what it does not mean. The New Testament uses a number of expressions to clarify what the church is. All of them have something essential to say. They complement one another, and together they give us a rich and many-sided picture of the biblical view of the church. Many of these biblical names for the church—as for example the vine and the branches, the temple building—strongly accentuate the fellowship and unity between Christ and the church. This is true in the highest degree of the term "Body of Christ." The unity between Christ and the church cannot be more forcefully maintained. But no matter how much Christ is one with his church, it is not a question of an identity but of a relationship. The church is not coterminous with Christ. What is said about Christ cannot without further ado be said of the church. Christ is the Savior who works in and through the church. The church cannot take the place of Christ or function as an intermediary between Christ and humanity. But the bond of union between Christ and the church is so solid and unbreakable that the term "Body of Christ" becomes adequate and something more than merely a more or less appropriate figure of speech. The church has life through Christ's life. We could apply the words of the Chalcedonian formula to the relationship between Christ and the church: united without division, without separation, but without confusion or change. Thus Christ and the church belong together. The church exists in and through Christ. *Christus-Kyrios* cannot be conceived of without his church. The two are an inseparable unity. If we say that the two are one, we are reminded that the Bible also speaks of the church as the "Bride" of Christ, an expression that is closely related to Body of Christ. The Letter to the Ephesians applies to Christ and the church the words that man and wife are to be one flesh, and adds: "This is a great mystery, and I take it to mean Christ and the church" (Eph. 5:31-32). The church and its members may be unfaithful. But Christ remains faithful. The

185

union he has established with his church remains indissoluble. He does not forsake it. He cares for it "that the church might be presented before him in splendor, without spot or wrinkle" (Eph. 5:27).

Christ is therefore in the most real sense the life-giving power in his church. He exercises this power through the means of grace in which he is actively present in his struggle against sin and death. Where the Word and the sacraments function, there the church which is one, holy, catholic, and apostolic is created, sustained, and grows. The guarantee that these attributes really belong to the church is the fact that the means of grace are functioning and that through them Christ makes men participants in the riches and fulness of salvation. Even if we speak here primarily of catholicity, it is obvious that both universality and continuity are rooted in the means of grace. They are clearly oriented toward universality. They do not stop at any boundary line and do not respect any human signs of limitation. "Here there cannot be Greek and Jew, circumcised and uncircumcised, barbarian, Scythian, slave, free man, but Christ is all, and in all" (Col. 3:11). The continuity is preserved in the same way. Men may have different opinions about the means of grace, but they remain nevertheless unchangeably the same, and the function they perform is the same in all ages.

It is clear from what we have said that the statement of the Creed about the one, holy, catholic, and apostolic church would be misinterpreted if the church were conceived of in a spiritualistic sense as an "invisible" church. In itself it is not strange that ideas of this kind appear, since the history of Christianity through the centuries bears abundant witness to features which are contrary to the honorific titles in the Creed. In reality there is also an element of truth in speaking about an invisible church because it is not possible to draw any visible boundaries around those who are the true members of the church of Christ, or who belong to the *congregatio sanctorum*. In this case the concept of invisibility is relatively justified, since it is only Christ himself who "knows his own." All attempts at a separation of this kind are contrary, not only to what is possible for human eyes to see, but also to the clear words of the Lord himself. Separation like this does not belong to this life, but to the time of "the last judgment."

But this does not mean that the church therefore is invisible. The one, holy, catholic, and apostolic church of the Creed is none other than the church of Easter and Pentecost which appeared once as a living, obvious, concrete reality, and which has since existed through centuries and generations. The great attributes belong to it in spite of all its obvious defects. The guarantee of this status is the fact that through the means of grace Christ continually realizes his work of redemption in and through his church. As surely as the victory of Christ is an eternally decisive victory, and as surely as he must reign "until he has put his enemies under his feet," no human sinfulness can destroy the exalted status of the church. But nothing unveils and judges its sinfulness and numerous defects more than this exalted status, nor can anything else so emphasize its inescapable duty to resist the destructive powers which prevent its unity, holiness, catholicity, and apostolicity from being realized in its life and work.

But just as the unity, holiness, catholicity, and apostolicity of the church are not properly recognized in a spiritualistic view of the church so these high attributes cannot be guaranteed through an institutional view of it. It cannot be denied, of course, that from the very beginning the church has had an institutional form. The church's office of the ministry is, as we have seen, not only a matter of convenience. The means of grace and the ministry of the means of grace belong inseparably together. The office of the ministry is a divine institution, and as such it is indispensable in the life of the church. But it is not the order that guarantees the effectiveness of the means of grace. On the contrary, it is the means of grace, effective in themselves, or rather the means of grace made effective through the continuing work of Christ, which necessitate and define the order. If the office of the ministry were to guarantee the effectiveness of the means of grace, the relationship between the means of grace and order would be reversed. On this account the guarantee that the church by nature is one, holy, catholic, and apostolic cannot be sought in the office of the ministry as such. Such a guarantee would be possible

only on the presupposition that the office is invested with infallibility, or, in other words, that the guidance of the Spirit is identified with the leadership of the hierarchy. But this identification
would give the order a position of lordship incompatible with
the fact that Christ alone is the Lord of the church.

Catholicity becomes petrified in institutionalism, in spiritualism
it vanishes.

19. *ECUMENICITY AND CATHOLICITY*

This central ecumenical question is concerned with the unity
of the church. But the question of the catholicity of the church
in its two fundamental aspects of universality and continuity also
becomes relevant in this connection.

When we speak about ecumenicity in this context, we think
primarily of those discussions between the churches connected
with faith and order. We will also have occasion to call attention
to the practical examples of ecumenicity which in modern times
have been expressed in the fact that certain churches have entered
into negotiations with the idea of establishing a common, united
church. Such negotiations, as we know, are carried on in various
parts of Christendom and in some instances have produced results. The most conspicuous result is the appearance of the Church
of South India, in which Anglicans, Presbyterians, Methodists, and
Congregationalists have united in a church with a common confession and organization.

While earlier attempts toward a common understanding within
Christianity were of a more private character, the modern ecumenical movement is so to speak official. It is the churches
themselves which through their representatives negotiate with one
another. The purpose which prompts the discussion of "Faith
and Order" has been interpreted in various ways. Under any
circumstances it is, however, a question of seeking to manifest
what has been known as "a visible unity." This does not mean
simply a united church. The negotiations toward union mentioned
above are apart from and quite independent of the discussions
on Faith and Order. When Faith and Order speaks of "a visible
unity," it is a question primarily of a manifestation of the fellowship or communion of churches with one another. To the extent

that this fellowship is conceived of as involving not only "faith" but also "order," it implies that full fellowship between the churches includes a mutual recognition of the ministerial office in the various churches. But the goal they are looking forward to is not uniformity. A few words from the report of the conference in Lund (1952) may be said to provide an adequate expression of what is meant. "We differ in our understanding of the character of the unity of the Church on earth for which we hope, though none of us looks forward to an institution with a rigid uniformity of governmental structure and all of us look forward to a time when all Christians can have unrestricted communion in Sacrament and fellowship with one another." [4]

In regard to "faith" the ecumenical discussions have been occupied with such things as the position of the Bible, confessions, sacraments, church, and worship life. I cannot discuss here to what extent these conversations have promoted catholicity. A couple of remarks may be made, however, in regard to the discussion on the sacraments. In these deliberations baptism has had a relatively inconspicuous place. This may be surprising since the different churches recognize each other's baptism, with the marked exception of the Baptist church. If somebody should claim that this universal position of baptism makes it unnecessary to enter upon a thorough discussion of it, I would say that exactly the opposite is true. The fact that this sacrament, which is fundamental for the church, occupies such a universally accepted position makes it imperative that the ecumenical movement take up the question of baptism for discussion, as it in fact has done in recent times, and seek to clarify what consequences *must* be drawn from the universal validity of baptism.

If baptism has been comparatively inconspicuous early in the ecumenical movement, the Lord's Supper has attracted that much more attention. To a great extent this has been due to the fact that the celebration of the Lord's Supper has not enjoyed the same universal recognition within the various churches as baptism. On this point the difficulties and hindrances in the way of full fellowship between the churches have been severely embarrassing. For a long time this has been manifested most clearly in

---

[4] *Lund, 1952,* pp. 21-22.

the many debates about "intercommunion" and the many factors concerned with this subject. Here we may simply record that these difficulties are connected with questions of order and doctrine. Some have demanded that a distinct and fully formulated doctrine of the Lord's Supper must be the condition for a common celebration of the Sacrament. The demand for a distinct form of order has been even more prominent in the debates. The real difficulties arise when a definite church order—the reference is to the episcopal—is invested with *fundamental* significance. We will return later to these questions.

The reason for not entering upon a closer investigation of the more or less official reports of the ecumenical conferences is that our chief interest in this book lies in a different direction. Our interest has been directed toward what has taken place and what is taking place *within* different communions. We are concerned with the inner front where traditional ways of stating the question, ways that have been securely held to for a long time, have been undergoing obvious shifts. It has been especially the Roman church that we have had in mind, which is natural since the subject of the book is Reformation and catholicity.

The picture of what is happening within the Roman church has proved to be full of contradictions. On the one hand, we found a much greater understanding of the intentions of the Reformation than has traditionally been the case, and a sometimes unreserved recognition of its fundamental religious point of view as this is seen against the background of the "decadence" of the Middle Ages. We also found a heavy emphasis on the authoritative position of the Bible and on its central significance for both worship life and Christian life in general. We noted the sharp criticism by the liturgical reform movement of the liturgical development—or rather deterioration—which since the Middle Ages has continued through the centuries, and also its energetic attempts to maintain the Sacrament as a means of grace in the full meaning of that term. We also saw that these attempts are associated with a biblically oriented view of the church where the idea of the church as the "Body of Christ" and *communio sanctorum* appears in the foreground. But at the same time we also found a conspicuous accentuation of the institutional and hierarchical view of the church, and in connection with this also a promulgation of doctrine without biblical foundation and, for that matter, without connection with—or even in opposition to—the tradition from the ancient church. Finally, in connection with the accentuation of the hierarchical view of the church we found a vigorous criticism of the so-called negations of the Reformation, which are supposed to stem from the "decadence" of the late Middle Ages.

With the exception of "Lutheranism" the presentation in this book has only in passing touched on what has happened or is happening within the other churches which are more or less closely related to the Reformation. It is obvious that here, too, significant changes are taking place in regard to traditional ways of stating the question. Discussions between Reformed and Lutherans have not ceased. But they have forsaken the old battle-fronts and started to move. A presentation of the Lord's Supper such as the Scottish theologian Torrance has given in *Intercommunion*[5] cannot be incorporated within the framework of the Reformation controversies; nor, to take another example, can the writings issuing from the Reformed monastery Taizé in France. The movement of liturgical renewal which at present is in progress within Reformed churches is well worthy of attention. In a book entitled *Liturgical Renewal,* the Strasbourg professor, J. D. Benoît, provides an instructive account of what is happening in the Reformed church of France.[6] The earlier negative attitude toward a fixed liturgy has been replaced by a conspicuously positive attitude to the common liturgical tradition from the ancient church, which is unquestionably an ecumenical feature.

I insert here a marginal remark. In this book we have again and again paid special attention to liturgical questions for good reasons. I will mention only two. The liturgy of a church has in reality a much greater significance than many have been willing to admit. It is indeed nothing more or less than the living and continuing confession of the respective communion. In addi-

[5] T. F. Torrance, "Eschatology and the Eucharist," *Intercommunion,* pp. 303ff.
[6] Jean D. Benoît, *Liturgical Renewal: Studies in Catholic and Protestant Development on the Continent,* trans. Edwin Hudson (London: S.C.M., 1958).

tion, the ecumenicity which expresses itself in liturgy goes considerably further than that which manifests itself at conferences where church leaders and theological experts are the chief participants. However important and decisive for ecumenical work such conferences may be, for obvious reasons it is difficult to influence the great masses in the congregations with this form of ecumenicity. Those who have participated in ecumenical work are well aware of the danger that ecumenicity may become a special concern of the "experts." A liturgical ecumenicity serves well to widen and extend the ecumenical base.

It is outside the plan of this work to investigate the many different attitudes toward catholicity appearing in the communions which have originated during recent centuries. Only a very brief observation will be made. I am sure that it would not be a mistake to say that individualistic and spiritualistic tendencies are on the point of being replaced in many quarters by a firmer view of the church, even within communions where these tendencies have previously been prevalent.

Ecumenicity and catholicity are closely related. Unquestionably ecumenicity has strongly contributed to making relevant the question of the attitude of each communion to the catholicity which according to the Creed is essential and inalienable. No church can justify its participation in ecumenical discussions without facing this problem seriously. To regard it as less essential or even a matter of indifference would mean an isolation from the universal, "catholic" church. We saw above that the catholicity of the Creed must be understood as a qualitative concept which primarily actualizes the universality and continuity of the church. Thereby the Creed enjoins a self-examination on the part of each individual communion. We have seen how just such a critical self-examination unreservedly has made its way even within that communion which otherwise has laid exclusive claim to catholicity for its own church, i.e., the Roman church. Self-examination is required of *all* churches. The criticism directed toward the defective catholicity of others may indeed have its significance. But much more important is the self-examination practiced within one's own communion. We will end this book, therefore, with a little "self-analysis" of the Lutheran church.

To begin with it is undoubtedly true that the Reformers wanted to maintain the church's catholicity. This is implicit in the very word "reformation." They wanted least of all to found a "new" church. The predominant and passionate desire of the Reformation was to bring to light the gospel which is "the greatest treasure" of the church, of the actual, historical, apostolic church, and to remove the elements which tended to set aside the gospel and obscure its significance. Its chief care was for the original and universal message entrusted to the church. But at the same time it was a question of continuity. Continuity cannot, of course, be conceived of as including everything that has grown up within Christianity during the centuries. No one can reasonably think of continuity in that sense. The emphasis must be placed on that which shows itself as being in line with and constituting a living continuation of what was originally given—that which, in other words, agrees with and so to speak "exploits" the apostolic message. The Reformation intended to maintain just such a continuity by appealing first and foremost to the authority of the Bible, but besides this also to the confessions of the ancient church and to the church fathers of the early centuries.

There can be no doubt about the *will* of the Reformation to certify its catholicity, or more correctly the catholicity of the church. It is a different question as to whether and to what extent this intention was realized in what happened. One of the chief purposes of this book has been to investigate this question.

The Reformation is a historical event and must be considered in its historical context. It cannot be understood if it is isolated and torn away from the situation in the church which produced it. To absolutize the decisions which were made at that time is impossible. Nor can we regard the definitions, formulations, and statements of problems as firm and unchangeable for all time. In the previous discussion we have seen many examples of how the ways of stating the question have changed. A discussion with other communions, both Roman and Reformed, can no longer be carried on simply by using arguments drawn from the controversies of the Reformation.

It cannot be denied, however, that within the Lutheran church there have been and still are tendencies to regard the confessional writings, and even Luther's statements and decisions, as sacrosanct. The Reformer has been the object of an apotheosis which he undoubtedly would have been the first to reject. Such an attitude has contributed to an isolation of Lutheranism. It has also caused the question of catholicity, with which the confession of faith confronts all the churches, to be shunted aside, and it has prevented Luther's voice from being heard within Christianity as a whole in a way commensurate with his magnificent ability and prophetic power to interpret the gospel of redemption in its clear and essential meaning. This tendency toward apotheosis has also resulted in attention being riveted to the polemical aspects of the Reformation and the negative statements made in regard to others. These negations, often stated radically in the heat of controversy, are also significant to be sure, but they are not of primary importance. They had significance only to the extent that they helped to clarify and protect the positive element which was the chief concern of the Reformation.

The Reformation, however, in no sense claimed infallibility either for its leaders or its statements or its decisions. On the contrary, in its confessional writings it has appealed to the Bible as the highest authority. No matter what value the men of the Reformation ascribed to their confessional writings, they maintained emphatically that these and everything in the life and work of the church must be subject to a continual re-examination with the Bible as absolute norm. In view of this fact we cannot regard the confessional writings as the final and definitive word without being disloyal to the clearly expressed principles of the Reformation. In the preceding sections we have heard Orthodox theologians say that the decisions of the ancient councils are indeed authoritative, but that they must be understood "historically and spiritually." This fundamental principle is reflected in the attitude of the Reformation. Faithfulness to the heritage of the Reformation does not imply slavery to the letter. The confessions of the Reformation have authority only because and insofar as they agree with the apostolic message of the Bible. To interpret the confessions "historically" means to pay due attention to the historical situation and its complications. To interpret it "spiritually" means to direct attention to the religious meaning of the confessions. These have been the intentions governing our investigation in this book. The purpose has not been to present an apology for everything that happened in the conflicts of the Reformation, and least of all for what has happened since in post-Reformation "development." The content of this book would seem to have given a clear indication that this was not the purpose. In the more than four hundred years since the Reformation, the Reformation confession has had a hard struggle to maintain its position. It has sometimes been reinterpreted in a subjective and individualistic sense that was foreign to the Reformation. It has also faced the threat of being smothered under a moralism diametrically opposed to what was the most important concern of the Reformation. The same struggle continues in the present. It is a struggle for the catholicity of the church.

What I have been interested in doing is primarily to understand the Reformation "spiritually," i.e., to explicate its religious meaning. This can be done only by paying attention to the context in which it stands. If it is separated from this context, it loses its meaning and becomes false teaching. I have tried to explicate the nature of this context in Chapter 2 by formulating the thesis: justification by faith alone is a statement concerning that redemptive act which the living Lord through the instrument of the means of grace continually performs in and through his church. In the previous sections we have seen what christological and ecclesiastical perspectives are included in the Reformation confession.

This confession is clearly biblical and stands in inseparable association with the confession of the ancient church. When in the previous pages I called attention to the significance of modern biblical research for our understanding of the Reformation confession, it does not mean that the Reformation has been modeled according to some pattern of modern biblical research. But it does mean that various re-interpretations or one-sided interpretations, which have in reality placed the Reformation in a context foreign to it, have yielded to an interpretation which does more justice to the actual, biblical context of the Reformation.

It has often been said that the Lutheran churches in their ecumenical participation have given a decisive—some even say one-sided—importance to *doctrina*. Behind this characteristic lies the fact that these churches are vividly conscious of the binding heritage of the Reformation. Their attitude is justifiable provided it does not involve the matter of a "new" confession or a specifically Lutheran confession, but emphasis on an aspect of the apostolic message and the biblical confession that cannot be surrendered. Understood in this sense the Reformation confession has not lost anything of its relevancy. It continues always to pose questions to all church communions, including the Lutheran. But this concern for the confession would be transformed into doctrinaire obstinacy if as a condition of church fellowship Lutherans were to demand that other churches accept the theological formulations in which the Reformation confession at one time had been promulgated. This attitude would be unreasonable simply because the same idea may be expressed theologically in various ways, and because the use of the same expression does not guarantee the same meaning. Under these circumstances it would be meaningless, for example, to demand an acceptance of the *term, "sola fide,"* as a condition for church fellowship.

The distinction we are making here between confession and *doctrina* has its background in the New Testament. Its confession of Christ is uniform, but it has been developed as "teaching" in different ways by biblical authors. The theme is the same, but it varies significantly for instance as Paul does from John. This is true all through the history of Christianity. In relation to the confession *doctrina* represents a fluid and elastic element. Its quality must be determined on the basis of the confession, first and foremost that of the New Testament, and second the confessions of the early church and the Reformation, since these guard the biblical message and protect it against erroneous and arbitrary biblical interpretations.

If therefore the apostolic message, or in other words the gospel, is constitutive for and qualitatively defines *doctrina,* the same is true also in regard to *liturgia* and *ordo*. Worship life as a whole is determined by the church's relationship to the crucified, risen, and living Lord, who in and through the means of grace continues his redemptive work in his church. In the same way *ordo* is something constitutive, an institution of the Lord for service to the church through the means of grace, and its character is therefore defined by its service to the means of grace. When the Augsburg Confession says that it is enough "to agree concerning the teaching of the Gospel and the administration of the sacraments," and adds that "it is not necessary that human traditions or rites and ceremonies, instituted by men, should be alike everywhere," it does not imply any indifference to *liturgia* and *ordo,* and still less antagonism to or contempt for continuity within the church in these respects. But the statement maintains freedom in the details of worship, and at the same time it rejects the idea that a certain definite order can claim infallibility in the administration of the means of grace or in general be designated as exclusively valid. No such claim can be made either by the papal, the episcopal, the presbyterian, or the congregational orders. None of these as such provide any sure guarantee against heresy, or for apostolic continuity. The only actual guarantee that the gospel will be preserved intact is to be found in the fact that "through the Word and sacraments, as through instruments, the Holy Spirit is given." It depends on the twofold promise of the Lord: the promise of the guidance of the Spirit, and the promise of his presence in his church always until the end of the age. But this does not mean that the questions of the constitution of the church and the form of the ministerial office are nonessential or matters of indifference, nor that the various church constitutions are of equal value. Decisions in these respects must be based upon what is learned from the history of the church, and they must be made not only in view of what may be expedient in the present situation but also with reference to what may serve and express the universality and continuity of the church. This point of view places serious demands on the Lutheran churches, but at the same time it gives them wide possibilities in ecumenical deliberations, even where it is a question of church union and the merger of several churches into one united church.

Finally we must say a word about the relationship of the Reformation to other churches. We may be reminded that Florovsky maintained that if a "Protestant" church wants to be consistent, it ought to regard itself as the only true church just like the Orthodox. A non-reformed church would from this point of view be an "un-true" church. This would be true on the condition that a reformed church regarded its confession as something new and the special property of the church in question. But the foundation for such a self-assertion is removed when the confession is regarded not as something new but only as an accentuation of one aspect of the biblical message. We have already quoted the well-known words of Luther to the effect that the gospel was found also under the papacy and that the Roman church is a holy church. These words remove all possibility of claiming that one's own church is the only true church. This statement has a fundamental significance of the greatest dimensions. Its profound meaning is the certainty that Christ performs his redemptive work through the means of grace, by grace alone, even where theological interpretations of what takes place are defective and inadequate. It is a comfort to know this, even for the Lutheran church.

INDEX

201